THE STRATEGIC SILENCE

THE STRATEGIC SILENCE

GENDER AND ECONOMIC POLICY

Edited by
Isabella Bakker

ZED BOOKS
in association with

THE NORTH-SOUTH INSTITUTE
L'INSTITUT NORD-SUD

The Strategic Silence was first published by Zed Books Ltd,
7 Cynthia Street, London N1 9JF, UK, and 165 First Avenue,
Atlantic Highlands, New Jersey 07716, USA, in association
with The North-South Institute/L'Institut Nord-Sud, Suite 200,
55 Murray Street, Ottawa, Canada K1N 5M3, in 1994

Copyright © The North-South Institute, 1994

Cover designed by Andrew Corbett
Typeset in Monotype Garamond by Lucy Morton, London SE12
Printed and bound in the United Kingdom
by Biddles Ltd, Guildford and King's Lynn

A catalogue record for this book is available from the British Library
US CIP data is available from the Library of Congress

ISBN 1 85649 261 3 Hb
ISBN 1 85649 262 1 Pb

The North–South Institute
The Institute is a Canadian non-profit corporation established
in 1976 to provide professional, policy-relevant research on the
'North–South' issues of relations between industrialized and
developing countries. The results of this research are made available
to policy-makers, interested groups and the general public to help generate
greater understanding and informed discussion of development questions.
The Institute is independent and non-partisan, and cooperates with a
wide range of Canadian, overseas and international organizations
working in related activities.

Contents

Contributors

Haleh Afshar is a social scientist at the University of York in the UK. She is co-editor with Carolyne Dennis of *Women and Adjustment in the Third World* and with Bina Agarwal of *Women, Poverty and Ideology in Asia*.

Isabella Bakker is a political economist at York University, Toronto, Canada. She is a contributor to Jenson, Hagen and Reddy (eds) *The Paradox of Women's Employment* and several other Canadian and international collections on women and labour markets, public finance and political economy.

Antonieta Barrón is an economist at the National University of Mexico researching rural women wage labourers.

Janine Brodie is a political economist at York University, Toronto, Canada. She is co-author of *The Politics of Abortion*, author of *The Political Economy of Canadian Regionalism, Women and Politics in Canada*, and contributor to the Royal Commission on Tax Reform.

Marjorie Griffin Cohen is a political economist at Simon Fraser University in Canada. She is the author of *Free Trade and the Future of Women's Work* and *Women's Work, Markets and Economic Development in Nineteenth Century Ontario*.

Diane Elson is an economist at the University of Manchester, UK. She is editor of *Male Bias in the Development Process* and the author of many papers on gender and adjustment for the UN, World Bank, and the Commonwealth Secretariat.

Barbara Evers is an economist currently at the University of Manchester, UK. She is the author of several studies on trade liberalization and employment in Indonesia.

Caren Grown is an economist and program officer for the MacArthur Foundation in Chicago, USA. She is co-author with Gita Sen of the

DAWN publication *Development, Crises and Alternative Visions*, and co-editor of a special volume of *World Development* (1990) on expanding income-earning opportunities for women in the developing countries.

Martha MacDonald is an economist at St Mary's University in Halifax, Canada. She has written extensively on women and the labour force, flexible specialization and gender.

Swapna Mukhopadhyay is an economist at the University of New Delhi, India. She is the author of the ILO publication *From Isolation to Empowerment: Women Home-Based Workers in the Less Developed Countries.*

Marjorie W. Williams is an economist, teacher and organizer in West Palm Beach, Florida, USA. She is the author of several articles on debt and gender.

Acknowledgments

The roots of this project go back to my days as a trainee at the Organization for Economic Co-operation and Development (OECD) for the Working Party on the Role of Women in the Economy. Subsequent encouragement from Maureen O'Neil and Françoise Core at Status of Women Canada allowed me to delve further into the question of women and economic development strategies. Maureen O'Neil, once again, asked me to take up this issue in my work with the North–South Institute.

Many friends and colleagues have contributed to my thinking on macro-economics and gender relations. First and foremost, I would like to thank the 'three Js' – Janine Brodie, Jane Jenson, and Jill Vickers. They have encouraged me from the beginning of my days as a student at Carleton and continue to be important intellectual touchstones. I would also like to thank Joanna Kerr of the North–South Institute for her intellectual contribution and her organizing skills. My colleagues at the Centre for Women's Development Studies in New Delhi have pushed me to explore similarities and differences in both issues and methodologies around gender and global restructuring. Diane Elson has been most generous with her time and intellectual support. I would also like to thank Lourdes Beneria, Gita Sen and David Gordon for encouraging me when it mattered. Finally, the biggest emotional and intellectual debt goes to Riel Miller who supports, encourages and tactfully criticizes.

Isabella Bakker
York University, Toronto, Canada

Preface

The struggle to transform women's place in society has moved from the courts to the counting house. Economics as well as law may be practised for the general good of women or quite the opposite. The Nairobi Forward-Looking Strategies understated the issue: 'While during the earlier part of the Decade the belief that economic growth would automatically benefit women was more widely shared, an evaluation of the experience of the Decade has shed considerable doubt on this over-simplified premise.' Women in both the South and the North saw that there were many holes in the promises of 'structural adjustment'. Women did seem to be the losers as deficits were attacked, public services cut and trade 'freed'. In October 1987 at the request of the Commonwealth Heads of Government, the Commonwealth Secretary-General convened an Expert Group to examine the impact of these measures on women. This was an important breakthrough in acknowledging that various approaches to economic policies did indeed affect men and women differently. The Expert Group did not mince words: 'The economic crisis of the 1980s, and the types of stabilization and adjustment measures taken in response to it, have halted and even reversed the progress in health, nutrition, education and incomes which women had enjoyed in developing countries during the previous three decades.'

How, then, should macro-economic policy be recast for the benefit of women? Can it be recast, if the reasons for differential impact are rooted in the multiplicity of women's roles, in the social constructs of their lives? Can we envisage and 'engender' macro-economic policy so that women may continue to improve their scandalously bad economic position? The North–South Institute set out to ask these questions in June 1992 through an examination of the economic policies that constitute today's economic-reform packages. Economic concepts and methodologies were explored. Case studies examined particular country and sectoral experiences. This seminar on the impact of macro-economic policies on women was the first event in a newly established research linkage between the North–South Institute and the Centre for Women's Development Studies in New Delhi. This book is drawn from the papers of participants in that seminar.

Maureen O'Neil
President, The North–South Institute

The Canadian International Development Agency (CIDA) provided funding support for this publication under the Canada–India Applied Economic and Business Policy Linkage Program, a programme of collaborative research managed by The Conference Board of Canada. Under the auspices of this programme, The North–South Institute, Ottawa, and the Centre for Women's Development Studies, New Delhi, collaborated in conducting the study 'Impact of Macro Policies on Women in the Period of Liberalization and Adjustment: Comparative Perspectives from Canada and India'.

INTRODUCTION:
Engendering Macro-economic Policy Reform in the Era of Global Restructuring and Adjustment
Isabella Bakker

The current restructuring of global economics has had profound effects on social, economic and political life in both developed and developing countries. There is widespread agreement on the elements of restructuring but little recognition of the gendered nature of the current process of structural and institutional transformation. Most treatments of structural change harbour a 'conceptual silence': the failure to acknowledge explicitly or implicitly that global restructuring is occurring on a gendered terrain. The dominant discourse[1] around restructuring remains cast in largely gender-neutral and aggregate terms, such as the imperatives of deficit reduction, international competitiveness, efficiency and export-led growth. The fact that structural adjustment and restructuring policies are largely formulated without consideration for asymmetrical relations of power based on gender leads to a silencing of women's experiences and strategies of resistance. For example, economic policies of trade liberalization and greater flexibility in shifting resources from one sector to another are premised on a commensurate mobility of individuals. But, in analysing this type of strategy, it is rarely if ever asked if the sexual division of labour makes it more difficult for women, relative to men, to switch from employment in non-tradeable sectors to tradeables production.

In more general terms, it is important to pose a series of gender-sensitive questions about the process of economic restructuring. Are there important constraints and costs of economic change that are usually neglected, such as the intra-household division of labour? What is the nature of the economic activity open to women relative to men? Is increased participation in the labour market by women a consequence of their disadvantaged position? Has restructuring merely achieved a sharing out of employment between larger numbers of women? Is global re-regulation restructuring and/or reinforcing women's generally segregated, unequal and tenuous place in the labour market?

Restructuring can be analysed as a series of cumulative and conjunctural crises in the international division of labour and the global distribution of economic and political power; in global finance; in the functioning of national states that are losing economic and political control of national economies; in the decline of the Keynesian welfare state and the established social contracts between labour, government and business; and in the increasing exploitation of marginal forms of labour performed by women, youth and minorities.

The emergence of the global assembly line and, in particular, the growth in the number of informal-sector workers and women's paid work is one of the centrepieces of global restructuring (Feldman, 1992: 1–2). In examining the global picture, we can discern a process of both *explicit* deregulation, an erosion or abandonment of formal regulations by legislative means, and *implicit* deregulation, through which remaining regulations have been made less effective due to inadequate implementation or systematic by-passing (Standing, 1989). Other aspects of this strategy include: export-led industrialization; the increasing fragmentation of the employment structure, particularly along gender lines; the shift, especially in the industrialized countries, from direct to indirect forms of employment such as sub-contracting from larger to smaller units; changing skill and job structures, including the trend toward skill polarization and greater reliance on external as opposed to internal labour markets. These patterns do not bode well for the gender division of labour within households and the labour force as the processes of economic and political globalization intensify.

Focusing on globalization may tend to obscure the national macroeconomic context.[2] However, as Elson suggests in her contribution (Chapter 2), there are good grounds for analysing the macro-level beyond the national context and focusing on the global level if policy reforms are to address the international system of trade, the investment and locational behaviour of transnational firms, and the impact of prolonged balance-of-payments imbalances. Furthermore, even though it is widely recognized that globalization does reduce the capacity of national governments to manage the economy to the same degree as under the postwar regime of Keynesian accommodation, it is equally important to bear in mind that the contours of the new global order are not yet firmly established. Hence, it is crucial to distinguish between, on the one hand, the neo-liberals' deterministic sense of system convergence that envisages the decline of nation states' political agency, and, on the other hand, the reality of national political economies continuing to strive to re-regulate and attenuate the disruption caused by the various forces of globalization.

'Convergence to what?' is a question that has not been definitively answered in the debate over which regulatory model can succeed in overcoming the severe social and economic turmoil that besets governments and citizens throughout the world. The resurgence of 'Keynesian realism' is, in practical terms, a sign that politicians and policy-makers are looking for alternatives to the structural adjustment policies of the 1980s. They are now urging that public investment strategies and more socially determined institutional change be at the forefront of restructuring initiatives (Freeman, 1992). Two forces are propelling the development of alternatives to Structural Adjustment Policies (SAP). First, SAP has failed to solve the primary economic challenges of improving productivity, employment and the standard of living. Second, SAP has now started to provoke organized resistance and a political counterattack as social and democratic institutions demand greater respect for collectively determined goals and values.

I. Gender-relations Analysis and Economic Policies of Restructuring

Systematically linking a gender-relations analysis to an economic-policy framework is a difficult task, given the blindness to gender issues in economic discourse. Gender relations can be defined in terms of the interplay between historical practices that are distinguished according to masculine and feminine (theories and ideologies, including religious ideas), institutional practices (such as state and market), and material conditions (the nature and distribution of material capabilities along gender lines). Gender relations are social constructions (social forces and historical structures) that differentiate and circumscribe material outcomes for women and men. This definition of gender relations recognizes that the interplay of race, class and sexuality underpins the form and structure of actual gender relations.

In this section, I develop three levels of argument. The first deals with the conceptualization of markets in standard economics. I argue that markets are institutions imbued with structural power relations and that these have an asymmetrical gender dimension to them. Any mechanisms that exclude or diminish benefits due to gender asymmetries need to be isolated in developing strategies for restructuring along democratic lines, that is, strategies that empower those who have insufficient access to or control over a sufficient number of resources. The second level focuses on macro-economics, a postwar field of economics based on Keynes that had some positive implications for gender disparities because it modified classical liberalism 'to make market behaviour consistent with social defence of more disadvantaged groups' and 'founded its legitimacy on consensual politics' (Cox, 1991: 341–3). However, Keynesian macro-economics still suffers from gender blindness because it largely ignores the unpaid labour of women in caring and reproduction tasks and the contribution of these to aggregate levels of economic activity and human development. These assumptions lead to a number of allocative and distributive gender-based consequences that disproportionately favour men and operate against women. At the most specific level, the third section deals with the attempt in the 1980s to re-regulate the global system through so-called structural adjustment policies that involve both micro- and macro-initiatives. Although structural adjustment measures in both the North and the South place greater emphasis on the role of individual economic agents in product and factor markets, there has been very little effort to distinguish the differential impact and feedback on a gendered basis. Perhaps, as Ingrid Palmer has noted, if one can demonstrate that gender issues impact on adjustment, then gender issues will become central to the discussion of economic efficiency and structural transformation (Palmer, 1992: 70).

1. Markets

Market-based regulation and coordination of disparate economic activities influence what kind of people we become through the shaping of preferences and values; they are, as Bowles suggests, 'social settings that foster specific types of personal development and penalize others' (Bowles, 1991: 13). The operation of markets, the formation of prices and the organization of production intrinsically rely on the operation of social and institutional norms that reflect the incompleteness of contracts. The non-market relations which surround and structure all markets become important in considering the terms on which people come to the market (Mackintosh, 1990). This is significant for gender-relations analysis because it introduces space for the notion that market goods and services are allocated through the political structure and social relations of markets, which may promote dominance and subordinacy between parties to an exchange. Markets may represent a positive development for groups previously excluded from economic independence; however, markets, like other institutions guided by social relations, are very likely to reflect and reify existing resource allocations and socially constructed gender divisions of labour that influence endowments.

The evaluation and analytical understanding of markets should include a consideration of the structural power of the market to discipline social relations, structure power and the access and control of resources, and the feedbacks on the process of human development. If markets are recognized to be as much political and cultural institutions as they are economic, then 'the standard efficiency analysis is insufficient to tell us when and where markets should allocate goods and services and where other institutions should be used' (Bowles, 1991: 11). Supplementing the analysis of market relations with insights from institutions operating at the meso level – that is, the structures which mediate between individuals and the economy such as public-sector agencies – would allow for social norms and networks to be introduced into the analysis of behaviour and decision-making. How norms and networks are gendered would then become a part of the analysis (see Elson, Chapter 2 in this volume).

Most economic discourse is dominated by neo-classical conceptions of markets that function on the basis of perfect competition. As a result, economic analysis is rooted, in its basic theoretical assumptions, in a gender-neutral abstraction of markets functioning with homogeneous labour inputs. However, markets do have a gender dimension to them. A gender-relations analysis focuses precisely on how market relationships that appear to be gender-neutral implicitly infer the male standpoint (Whitehead, 1979; Elson, 1993). As Elson puts the point:

> Being a worker, or a farmer, or an entrepreneur, does not overtly ascribe gender; but women and men have very different experiences as workers, farmers and entrepreneurs; and the supposedly gender-neutral terms 'worker', 'farmer', 'entrepreneur', are imbued with gender implications. In fact, the 'worker' or 'farmer' or 'entrepreneur' is most often taken to be a man – creating male bias in both economic analysis and economic policy. (Elson, 1992: 2)

This bias is circumscribed and shaped primarily by the way in which a society organizes the interrelationship between paid work and raising children. Most people (mainly women) engaged in child-rearing do not have an independent entitlement to resources and are dependent on others or welfare-state arrangements to meet their needs. Markets operate without recognizing that the unpaid work of reproduction and maintenance of human resources contributes to the realization of formal market relations (see Elson, Chapter 2 in this volume, for a detailed elaboration). For the economist Ingrid Palmer, women's unpaid work in reproduction and family maintenance can be seen as a 'tax' that women are required to pay before they can engage in income-generating activity (Palmer, 1991). She argues that gender relations based on a hierarchy of resources and unequal terms of exchange between women and men lead to resource misallocations that can be viewed as 'gender-based market distortions'. She concludes that women do not enter the market with the same resources and mobility (that is, they cannot compete equally) because of the reproductive labour tax and gender-based distortions in resource allocation. For women, access to markets is limited because of the reproduction tax and because of their unequal terms of participation in markets, relative to men (Palmer, 1992: 74).

The market offers limited independence, given the lack of adequate child care and the type of work available to those who have the task of child care (Bakker, 1988; OECD, 1992). Typically, welfare states in the OECD countries do not rest on unconditional entitlements and are frequently constructed around a definition of citizenship that rests on employment or a continuous stream of income above the poverty level (Lewis and Ostner, 1990; Gordon, 1990). Such definitions reinforce a male standard of political and economic citizenship, one that does not recognize the unequal division of unpaid work. Nancy Folbre has demonstrated how distinct patterns of gender bias in social entitlements in Latin America and sub-Saharan Africa reflect a limited and unequal definition of citizenship. In both these regions, programmes such as basic pensions and family allowances are not targeted at all citizens, nor at those who are most needy; instead, they are aimed at a subset of male wage-earners (Folbre, 1992). Unequal economic citizenship, often shaped by the state as much as the market (see Brodie, Chapter 3 in this volume), reinforces the unequal terms of market participation for women. A large body of feminist research on advanced capitalist welfare states comes to similar conclusions. In this research, distinctions are made between different welfare-state regimes – on the basis of the differing proportions in which the household, the market, the state, firms and the Church provide services – and how they contribute to women's working and living conditions. These differences are determined, in part, by the society's attitude to women's participation in paid work – whether the methods of welfare-state income transfers or services are centred on individuals or households (Langan and Ostner, 1991). Such distinctions are important for the material conditions of different groups of women. However, all rest on the contingent citizenship of women: as events of the 1980s have shown, policies that are 'woman friendly' can be taken away even though they are based on legitimate claims.

Limiting welfare states in the core countries and future developments for welfare in the newly industrializing countries is an added dimension that will shape women's economic and political citizenship in the new global order. Whilst reprivatization discourse[3] is framed in terms of the reshaping of citizenship in general, via the denial of claims to universal social rights from the state, there are specific gender-based elements to its reconstruction.

2. Macro-economics

In the 1980s, budget deficits were pre-eminent as the most symbolic macro-policy variable. Through the concerted effort of IMF stabilization policies in the South and neo-liberal policy pressures in the OECD states, expenditure restraint, rather than revenue-raising measures, became the major policy initiative for dealing with deficits. In their study, Cornia and Stewart note that 'IMF stabilization policies [were] invariably associated with a target reduction in ... deficits, with the prime emphasis on attaining this reduction through expenditure cuts rather than tax increases'. The emphasis on demand-restraint policies has aggregate impacts as well as specific consequences for gender relations. The contractionary effect of demand restraint is due to cuts in government spending and reductions in real wages. The immediate employment effects are felt in the formal sector through reductions and spill-over effects occurring in terms of greater demand for informal-sector employment. In both the North and the South, participation rates for women have tended to rise or remain stable as women try to bolster household income (see Williams, Chapter 5 in this volume). This is often in the context of greater demands on their time for maintenance and reproduction of human resources (for example, food preparation, child care). Furthermore, government cuts in health and education have led to a deterioration in the quality of life for women and their families, particularly in the developing countries (Stewart, 1992: 27–9). In addition, the introduction of user fees for education and health care serves to bias investment away from female human resources (Palmer, 1992: 78). Stewart cites the examples of Bendel State in Nigeria, where the introduction of fees for primary schools led to a one-third decline in the enrolment rate, and the introduction of health charges in Ghana, which resulted in a decrease in clinic attendance. Both trends influence the ability to maintain and reproduce human resources. In the OECD countries, cuts in public services have been supplemented by an emphasis in some countries on 'injecting competition into the provision of public services'. Voucher systems for some educational and health services are just one example of the reconstitution of the form of state activities that is currently underway.

Engendering macro-economic policies

The phrase 'engendering macro-economic policies' refers to a twofold analytical process. First, a gendered analysis of macro-economics examines the differential consequences of macro-economic policy reforms for women and men, given the emphasis on paid activity and the neglect of reproduction. Second, there is the important feedback of gender-based social, economic and political differences on macro-economic decisions and outcomes. The primary focus here is on the former link between macro-policy/economic change and gender differentials.

In a way that is similar to the basic conceptualization of markets, the analytical foundations of macro-economics are not linked to a gender-relations analysis. Emerging out of the postwar acceptance of Keynesian, demand-oriented economic policies, macro-economics is preoccupied by aggregate measures of economic change, such as output levels, their fluctuations and relationship to rates of growth, unemployment and inflation, the budget surplus/deficit, levels of government expenditure and taxation, the changing balance between different sectors of the economy, monetary and exchange-rate policy. As Elson states, 'Women do not appear – but neither do men' (1992: 3).

Despite the absence of people at the level of macro-economic theory and measurement, there are, nevertheless, built-in assumptions about the following: the individual, who is, paradoxically, both a commodity and a rational economic person;[4] the determinants of the level and pattern of economic activity; human resources, how they are allocated to production, and how they are reproduced and maintained. These assumptions include the non-problematization of reproduction (it is outside of economic inquiry and hence automatic or 'natural'), the view that women's labour is infinitely elastic (able to stretch in times of restraint, contract in prosperity), and the belief that the switching of resources occurs because all factors have relatively equal mobility (Elson, 1987). In this sense, all the costs and benefits of resource reallocations, and their asymmetrical impact on gender relations, may not be fully captured. Furthermore, the dialectical relationship between market and non-market activity is left out of policy-reform planning.

Methods of state intervention

The interdependence of market and non-market activity is developed in the following consideration of macro-policy, which delimits potential gender asymmetries due to an exclusive focus by policy-makers on aggregate demand and supply. This has consequences for policy outcomes, and for aggregate levels of human development (see UNDP, 1992).

Taxation   At the aggregate level of total revenue raised, there are no obvious differentials by sex. Yet, once taxes are decomposed into direct (income) and indirect (consumption, VAT), several gender effects can be discerned. For example, indirect taxes are recognized as having a greater impact on women because of their universal role as managers of the household consumption budget (Edwards, 1980), whereas direct-income taxes fall more on men because of their greater access to employment and higher incomes (OECD, 1985). As Joekes has noted, there is very little research on this topic (she cites Beneria and Roldan's 1987 study of homework and subcontracting in Mexico City), noting that 'The impact on women of increased expenditure taxes may be indirect, via their efforts to generate extra income through increases in paid labor time, or to increase the consumption value of purchased goods by devoting more unpaid labor time to their processing, but in either case it is costly in terms of women's total effort' (Joekes, 1988: 9). The almost universal trend to value-added taxes in the 1980s has also been recognized as a regressive policy initiative from the vantage point of the poor and women who, in global terms, constitute the majority of the poor. Consumption taxes disproportionately impact on the lower-income groups who pay a larger chunk of their earnings through this tax.

Finally, as has already been noted, Palmer has developed the notion of a 'reproduction labour tax' or overhead which women must pay before they can engage in income-generating or expenditure-displacing activities. She argues that, 'Like all taxes it influences the allocation of resources, in this case in the form of penalising women's labour time in other activities which are both remunerative and more open to productivity increases. Resources in reproduction are not properly costed (and therefore not properly used)' (1992: 79). Women's reproductive work in the household is a tax because women are supplying a resource, the replacement of the present labour force, free to society. Palmer makes a comparison with employers who draw on their depreciation accounts when capital equipment has to be replaced; this has direct implications for lower profits and company taxes. As she notes, 'Biology and culture oblige mothers to bear almost the entire cost of a depreciation account for the labour force. Therefore when women return use values to their families with their domestic work it is because society has imposed upon them the responsibility for this particular (labour force) depreciation account' (1992: 80). Restructuring and adjustment policies can be directly linked to this labour tax on women since cuts in public social expenditure increase it and lead to a further distortion of resource allocation. Similarly, social investment in reproductive work via state-funded child care and maternity leave, for example, or via an employers' tax, would shift the tax from women to society and/or to all employers.

Expenditure Assessing the impact of expenditure policies on gender is a highly complex task due to the vast range of programmes, types of spending and the complexities introduced by the reform of trade regimes (see Cohen, Chapter 7 in this volume, on NAFTA). From an exclusively macro-economic vantage point, the central concern is the impact of shifts in aggregate demand and the subsequent changes in output, employment and prices. Undoubtedly, as explained above, a larger or smaller deficit will work its way through the economy in ways which change not only the macro-aggregates but also the relative economic status of men and women.

However, any effort to understand the way in which decisions to alter aggregate demand are not gender-neutral must go beyond the employment, output and price effects to contend with the highly differentiated impact of shifts in expenditure levels and priorities directly on women. The starting point for this more disaggregated analysis is naturally a taxonomy of state spending. Approaches to defining the different aspects of state expenditure range from modest accounting frameworks to full-fledged functional breakdowns. Four major government spending functions are usually isolated: (i) 'pure' public-goods provision (defence, government administrative services); (ii) merit goods (education, health, housing); (iii) income maintenance and other transfers; and (iv) general economic services (OECD, 1985; 1991b). I offer a disaggregation of several of these expenditure categories, which is by no means comprehensive; rather, the intention here is to use examples to illustrate the meaning of a gender-aware analysis.

(a) Public employment[5] Public-sector wages are an important instrument of macro-economic policy in the dual sense of setting the *de facto* standard for the private sector as a comparator and influencing the total demand for labour in the economy. Also, public-sector employment influences the level of aggregate demand, thereby acting as a built-in stabilizer. The OECD cites a strong correlation between women's labour-force activity and the size and growth of the public sector (OECD, 1993: 11). Cuts in public-sector expenditure may be particularly damaging to women's labour-market position, given that the public sector provides relatively more job opportunities and higher salaries for women than does the private sector. In the public sector there is less vertical segregation (concentration of women in low positions) and greater horizontal occupational segregation (concentration of women in few occupations). Also, the majority of these jobs offer better employment protection and social security. However, recent developments in public-sector employment, keeping in mind the variation across OECD countries, indicate a trend towards greater reliance on precarious part-time positions and lower wages compared to the high-growth period of the public sector.

(b) Capital expenditures (economic services) Capital expenditures refer to investments in fixed assets such as infrastructure. Salaries are the main component of operating costs, and therefore raise similar issues to those outlined in the previous section on public-sector wage bill cuts. Capital expenditures tend to have greater short-term positive employment impacts on men given their employment concentration in construction, engineering and other infrastructure-related trades. In the longer term, however, infrastructure spending on schools, hospitals, transportation, water and sewage systems can also have a profound effect on both women's tasks in the household sector and their labour-market position.

(c) Subsidies (economic services) Subsidies often take the form of compensation for the cost of price controls on certain selected products, such as food and fuel; these tend to comprise a significant chunk of public expenditure in developing countries. Joekes notes that:

> Insofar as those effects [price controls] discriminate against women, the higher the level of subsidy, the worse the effect against poor women, in terms of loss of benefit. On the other hand, there may be an absolute, if not proportional, gain to women through larger subsidies, insofar as the total subsidy represents a higher contribution to total income of the poor. The gain will be greater if a larger subsidy represents an increased supply of price controlled good, rather than a lowering of price, since that will tend to reduce the opportunities for the development of a secondary market in the good, at mark-up prices. (Joekes, 1988: 10)

In the OECD, it is useful to distinguish between compensatory and complementary subsidies. Compensatory subsidies are intended to cushion the social consequences of structural change, whereas complementary subsidies are actually put in place to help stimulate structural change (Mosley and Schmid, 1992). A gender-aware approach to subsidies would look at the sectoral composition of subsidies, relating this to the gender-based composition of employment in that sector. Where is structural change being stimulated? In what regions? Who is being employed via the funding of subsidies? Where is structural change occurring? What kind of compensatory subsidies are in place? Who is benefiting? For example, the subsidizing of the domestic aluminium or steel industries via cheap energy may benefit male workers in that industry. Another example would be tax versus cash subsidies in the area of training (public vocational training versus cash incentives to employers): which industries and sectors benefit from these (for example, in terms of high value added)? What is the gender composition of the sectors and train-ing participation?

(d) Service delivery (merit goods)   Service or programme delivery, such as improving the level of human capital (through education, training and health care) and technology, relate to the structural aspects of macro-economic policies. Cutbacks in the delivery of services are part of the effort to reduce government spending and deficits and have been a feature of structural adjustment programmes' attempt to free labour for the production of tradeables. However, such cuts have implications for both employment and unpaid domestic labour. As Elson observes, 'If fewer of the services required for the sustenance of human resources are provided by the public sector, then women have to make up the shortfall' (Elson, 1991: 177).

Debates about the efficiency and cost-effectiveness of public-sector provision of goods and services, especially welfare-state merit goods and transfer payments, have dominated the discussion of restructuring the public–private sector relationship in the OECD. This partly reflects the movement away from equity to efficiency and competitiveness con-cerns. However, pessimistic views of the welfare state's impact on international competitiveness and the necessary downward pressure on levels of social protection that such a view prescribes, remain subjects for further empirical research and debate (Mosley and Schmid, 1992). This debate, too large to cover here, should allow for a consideration of alternative regimes for the provision of public services. A gender-aware approach to the restructuring of state-provided services would include alternatives from the viewpoint of the users of services and be directed at the goal of facilitating human-resource development. In other words, a primary consideration for the restructuring of public-sector services should be the extent to which such restructuring will lessen the burden that women are asked to contribute (a reduction in the 'reproductive labour tax') before they are able to enter paid employ-ment. Micro-studies that look at intra- and inter-household changes are necessary to give a fuller picture of the gendered effects of macro-economic policies. In addition, further empirical work is needed to reveal fully the state's role in shaping or reducing women's unpaid reproductive burden.

(e) Transfers (income transfers and benefits)   Income transfers are the major means by which governments attempt to meet their redistributive objectives. Four major categories of transfers in the OECD are: old age and disability benefits; unemployment benefits; family allowances; and sickness and maternity benefits. Demographic, fiscal and political pres-sures have all influenced this area of spending during the 1980s. The shift from equity to efficiency concerns, plus the fiscal crisis of many OECD states, have contributed to the process of restraint and restriction of eligibility to various transfer programmes. The differentiated consequences, for men and women, of transfer changes would need to take into account all these factors. The extent to which individual economic security depends on transfers (for example, old-age benefits versus private pensions) also needs to be distinguished along gender lines. From OECD research, we do know that unemployment benefits and temporary-sickness and maternity benefits increased little in real terms in the 1980s (OECD, 1991b: 173). In some cases, unemployment benefit per recipient increased relative to per-capita gross domestic product as eligibility was reduced. The EC seems to confirm that there may be a gendered dimension to eligibility reductions: it is noted that in 1989 for the whole of the European Community, 26 per cent of women jobseekers and 34 per cent of male jobseekers received unemployment benefits or welfare (Commission of the European Communities, 1992: 33).

Monetary and exchange-rate policies   Monetary policy is how government influences the rate of interest in order to regulate the level of investment, output, employment and other macro-economic outcomes. A range of financial policies also influence the conditions of access to credit. There is a great deal of debate in the economics literature about the manner in which monetary-policy tools actually influence the economy. There are equally diverse opinions regarding the relationship between interest rates, one of the primary monetary targets, and investment. At a macro-level the impact of monetary policies on gender status and asymmetries is translated through the same aggregate variables as fiscal policy. However, when considered in terms of the specific mechanisms used to conduct monetary macro-policy there is a wide range of distinct effects on women and men.

For example, monetary policy often targets exchange rates and is used by governments to promote (by reducing the value of the currency) or discourage (by pushing up the value of the currency) exports, and hence influence the level and type of domestic production activity and employment. Monetary policy also targets interest rates, often with the aim of reducing inflation by making it more expensive to borrow money. Uncovering the gender dimensions of interest-rate targets involves an examination of the immediate effects of interest rates on different types of economic activities plus a careful consideration of the secondary consequences due to changes in the cost of living. It is with this latter impact that non-production activity needs to be surveyed, as cost-cutting is often absorbed by women's increased labour in the household and in the care-providing sector. Women's disadvantaged position vis-à-vis credit markets, both in terms of insufficient collateral and the institutional procedures of credit-lending agencies, implies that changes in monetary policy are likely to have differential impacts on women and men.

Engendering an analysis of monetary policy and tracing the differential impacts of interest- and exchange-rate targets encompasses a large part of the analytical task surrounding structural adjustment and restructuring policies. As a number of studies make clear, the burdens imposed by structural adjustment policies that combine high interest rates with cuts in government spending (as part of a strategy to reduce deficits) fall disproportionately on poorer urban and rural women and children, since they are the more vulnerable groups in society (Cornia, Jolly and Stewart, 1987; Elson, 1991).

Table 1.1, at the end of the chapter, summarizes the three areas of macro-policies (taxes, spending, monetary), contrasting standard economic analysis with the gender-relations dimension. Also shown are two other types of discretionary policy: market-regulating and social policies that influence how male and female economic opportunities are structured. From the perspective of aggregate economic performance, social policies are treated as automatic stabilizers. Shifting from the macro- to the micro-perspective, social policies influence some key gender differences such as asset holdings and the scope of individual decision-making in the labour market. Market-regulating policies reflect a micro-focus that came to the forefront in the 1980s with criticisms that markets were imperfect because government, unions or oligopoly induced distortions. Market-regulating policies reflect the attempt by governments to set the operating parameters in the land, labour, financial and product markets. Often the effect of these policies is to distinguish markets even further into regulated and unregulated parts. At the same time, the directness of the gender bias of market-regulating policies will tend to vary depending on the market in question. A major focus of structural adjustment policies has been to deregulate or dismantle government intervention in financial, social, labour and product markets. These issues are treated in more detail in the following section.

3. Structural adjustment and restructuring

In the 1980s, both developed and developing countries undertook policies that were targeted at the goals of stabilization and adjustment. These initiatives represented a break in the postwar macro-economic Keynesian consensus on the role of government in maintaining full employment and a shift toward the classical Smithian position of 'the night watchman state'. In attempting to define structural change or restructuring, one runs up against a number of different concepts, measurements and approaches. For standard economics, structural change at the most basic level involves a change in the composition of something – the economy, a sector, region or firm, for example. Most conventional economic analysts distinguish structural change in industrial structures from cyclical shifts in the composition of output, employment and trade. A standard account is offered by the OECD, which isolates two aspects or dimensions of structural change:

> Compositional structural change refers to changes in the industrial composition or profile of an economy: changes in the output or employment shares accounted for by different industries, for example, or changes in the mix of factor inputs used by industries. Its main characteristic is that it examines individual industries; the capital and labour inputs they use; and the way in which industries are connected to one another, both domestically and internationally. Its strength is that it provides a detailed picture of how the structure of an economy and its interlinkages have evolved over time. Its weakness is that it points only indirectly to policy actions ... Institutional structural change is concerned with the behaviour of labour and financial markets, the traded goods market, and the operation of the public sector ... The characteristic of institutional structural change is that it examines broad markets not necessarily restricted to any one industry and is concerned with deviations from competitive market behaviour ... The strength of institutional structural change indicators is that they are directly related to policy actions. Their weakness is that they are often difficult to derive and in many cases must be obtained as the result of modeling, itself an indirect process. (OECD, 1992: 167–8)

Over the last decade, in recognition of the compositional and institutional changes taking place, a broad range of governmental and quasi-governmental organizations shifted toward policies of demand-side restraint (stabilization) and supply-side flexibility (structural adjustment). For example, in the early 1980s the World Bank, partially in response to international balance-of-payments problems, shifted from loans targeted for particular projects to loans tied to changes in macro-economic policy. Stabilization policies aim to constrain aggregate demand, using the traditional demand-side fiscal and monetary macro-policy tools, including taxes, spending, monetary and exchange-rate policy. Stabilization policies aim to deal with balance-of-payments problems and inflation by inducing a slowdown in the economy by cutting aggregate demand. Cuts in government spending on services, salaries and investments are advocated as a method for realizing a more stable and efficient economy. Structural adjustment policies are seen as complementary to stabilization with an emphasis on supply-side measures at the micro-level. Naturally, policies that operate at the behavioural level of the market will vary according to the specific economic characteristics of a nation. The OECD notes that:

Despite the diversity of structural adjustment policies, a comparison of the different programmes shows that they are all inspired by the same philosophy: the value of the *liberalization of trade*, both domestic and foreign, and in some cases that of the privatization of parapublic enterprises to increase the efficiency of the economy. (1992: 13)

Structural adjustment policies influence gender relations on a number of fronts by altering the relationships between the productive and reproductive spheres, and the state's role in redefining and expanding the 'private'. The invisibility of shifting costs from the paid to the unpaid economy is a significant but hidden element of restructuring and adjustment (Elson, 1991). Structural adjustment and stabilization packages offer a good example of a series of macro-/micro-economic policy initiatives that were formulated without linking the restructuring of the global political economy to realignments in the public and private economic and political space.

Most research on the gendered dimensions of restructuring has been conducted in developing countries, where the effects of adjustment have been severe. In Mexico, for example, inflation reduced real incomes, and the price increases that followed the devaluation of the peso resulted in a decrease in the urban real minimum wage of 47 per cent between 1982 and 1988 (Beneria and Feldman, 1992). However, a disproportionate burden is placed on women because of the sexual division of labour which means that deep cuts in household budgets and demand-reducing policies such as cuts in public services (education, health) or goods and services subsidized by the government (electricity, public transport, basic foodstuffs) increase pressures on those who administer the household on a daily basis. The need to stretch the pay-cheque in order to meet basic needs, and the anxiety and conflicts over decisions about which items to cut from diets and household consumption often means an intensification of domestic work: more cooking, changes in purchasing habits; and so on (Beneria and Roldan, 1987; Joekes, 1988). In theory, economic adjustment implies that the market should fill the vacuum left by state-expenditure reductions; however, switching resources into tradeables from non-tradeables means that resources concentrated on the production and maintenance of human resources are not part of the 'adjustment' predicted by the theory.

To take another example of the gender implications of SAP, it is widely recognized that restructuring means a relative increase in the proportion of women exposed to direct market forces (whether as workers, traders or consumers). The feminization of work has been one consequence for some countries of the re-regulation of their political economy (Standing, 1989). Feminization of the labour force is a process whereby women, often paid lower wages, take jobs formerly filled by men. The increasing share of service-sector employment in many OECD countries also shifts employment towards job categories dominated by women. This suggests that the impacts of restructuring may be mitigated through employment gains for women and may have positive side effects, such as favouring the activity of women's organizations (Waylen, in Afshar and Dennis, 1992). Barrón (Chapter 10 in this volume) supports such a view in the case of Mexican women rural wage workers who are engaged in the expanding export sector of vegetable and fruit production. Evers (Chapter 8 in this volume) demonstrates how changing incentives under adjustment, in conjunction with trade liberalization, have stimulated contradictory dynamics within the textile industry in Indonesia. There has been an increased demand for female labour; but, with higher productivity and changing technology, female-operated handlooms have been increasingly displaced. The experience in many of the newly industrializing countries suggests that export-oriented restructuring in the labour market has disproportionately affected women workers, who are paid at or below subsistence and without protection (Commonwealth Experts Group, 1989; Cornia, Jolly and Stewart, 1987; Haddad, 1991; Rubery, 1988; Vickers, 1991; Jenson, Hagen and Reddy, 1988; Joekes, 1988; Brown and Pechman, 1987). In addition, there is evidence that women workers are disproportionately represented in a number of sectors like textiles, where there has been an intensification of work effort and a deterioration of working conditions due to the competitive pressures in both labour and product markets arising out of trade liberalization and deregulation.

II. Outline of this Volume

All of the contributors to this volume share the view that by silencing the experience of one half of a gendered society we are obscuring or excluding them from policy frameworks. Each chapter is an attempt to expand the discourse around restructuring and to put into question the exclusion of multiple actors and multiple levels or sites of decision-making.

Part I, Conceptual Silences and New Research Strategies, brings together a number of contributors who consider current macro-economic methods and policies, and who propose elements of a more gender-aware economics. Some fall within the boundaries of the neo-classical framework; others suggest an epistemological break away from the homogenizing thrust of Western economism toward 'multiple objective worlds' with their own validity (see Ekins and Max-Neef, 1992, for a discussion on new advances in economic science and understanding).

Diane Elson has been a pioneer in the area of gender analysis and development economics. In her chapter, Elson links the concepts of the macro, meso and micro used by orthodox and critical economists to a gender-relations analysis. She demonstrates how male bias is constituted at the micro-, meso- and macro-levels, that is, at the level of the family, mediating institutions and monetary aggregates. In particular, Elson examines how social institutions and monetary relationships which are not intrinsically gendered become the bearers of gender. At the meso level of the operation of markets, firms and public-sector agencies, relationships are gendered via the social norms and networks which are functional to their operation. Whilst such customs (hierarchical organization and the social cohesion of men, for example) that fill the gaps in incomplete contracts may be functional for economies, the benefits are very unequally distributed and reflect the hegemony of the powerful. Hence, new markets and firms that are the by-products of state restructuring and economic policy reform cannot rest on shared social understandings that will merely initiate new instances of male bias. At the macro-level, the incompleteness of money's mobilizing power allows for an introduction of gender relations. Elson notes that money mobilizes human effort via prices and wages yet it is not able directly to mobilize all the resources for the reproduction and maintenance of human labour power; a feminist critique of economic-policy reform at the macro-level would suggest that the reproductive economy cannot be taken for granted, that women's labour is not infinitely elastic in response to adverse macro-changes and the necessity to continue to meet basic needs of families and communities. Male bias is constituted in this one-sided view of the macro-economy which focuses on monetary aggregates and ignores the human aggregates of the reproductive economy (such as population, health, education). Overcoming male bias in macro policy-reform programmes would require targets for human development aggregates and complementary policy instruments, and a specification of whose rights (male and female) will be changed and how.

Janine Brodie, in her contribution, challenges us to go beyond our thinking about the gendered effects of restructuring as being limited to the labour market or production alone, because this process entails a shift in boundaries both between the state and the economy as well as between the so-called 'public' and 'private' spheres. Restructuring, she argues, involves a realignment of the social, political and economic through the state's constituting and reconstituting gender relations during periods of profound structural change. One consequence for North America of this particular round of restructuring is the erosion of the public and the simultaneous valorization of the private. This has disrupted and displaced both the sites and objects of political struggle (that is, the welfare state) for women and all disadvantaged groups. Brodie argues that most of the discourse of globalization has been phallocentric, because it represents highly gendered social agents or processes in terms of universals and genderless abstracts such as 'worker', 'entrepreneur', 'efficiency' and 'competition'. Uncovering the phallocentric nature of restructuring discourse is, however, only a first step; Brodie notes that a feminist analysis 'must begin with the premise that restructuring represents a struggle over the appropriate boundaries of the public and private, the constitution of gendered subjects within these spheres and ultimately, the objects of feminist political struggle.' Reconstitution of the private (what Fraser calls a reprivatization discourse) has manifested itself through attempts to repatriate the economic and the social to their former domestic enclaves and thereby to revitalize the hetero-patriarchal family. For Brodie, the disappearance of the structural and economic foundations of the Keynesian welfare state may be a moment for the women's movement in industrialized liberal democracies to assert a model of social citizenship and social reproduction that is free of previous patriarchal underpinnings.

The last two contributions to Part I focus on two relatively under-conceptualized areas of research. Caren Grown raises some preliminary questions for policy-makers pursuing the goals of sustainable economic growth, fulfilment of basic needs, and the development of healthy populations. She urges us to link discussions of structural adjustment and restructuring to a new understanding of population and economic growth that takes into account the interdependence of such policies. Grown reviews several of the current approaches to population and demographics before considering the future prospects for population programmes. She warns that financial pressures in both donor and recipient countries suggest fewer resources to meet the goals of population planning. At the same time, macro-economic policy packages directed at structural economic change may have a greater influence on population parameters than traditional policies directed at fertility control.

Marjorie Williams offers a reinterpretation of two key concepts within economics: productivity and efficiency. Bringing gender into our discussion of these concepts will lead to a reformulation of economic inputs and outputs and will make visible much of women's work that has previously been only an implied element of economic analysis. The hidden dimensions of the productivity slowdown and the global restructuring of production are linked to the feminization-of-work thesis. Williams discounts the view that women's labour has been responsible for declining national productivity, and sees it, rather, as a source of dynamic comparative advantage. This conclusion is reinforced by Cohen's evaluation of North American free trade in Part II.

Part II offers reflections on state, economy and household relations from the perspective of empirical research and case studies. Despite the specificities of each case study, contributors have distilled from the concrete situation observations about method and key questions for inquiry. Martha MacDonald's case study of restructuring in the fishing industry in Atlantic Canada is an important example of how the inclusion of gender and households (which reflect both co-operation and conflict) facilitates a clearer understanding of changes in the labour process and the transformation of an industry. Revealing the gendered nature of restructuring in the industry and the labour process allows MacDonald to engage with the broader debates on flexible specialization. She concludes that, while increased flexibility of capital can be consistent with increased control over workers, the labour changes in the fisheries have worsened conditions for the workers, especially the increasingly feminized fish-plant processing workforce. Men's jobs have benefited more from functional flexibility and have been less affected by technological changes. Restructuring of the industry has also brought about new household and community relationships, which are discussed in the latter part of the chapter.

Marjorie Cohen's broader consideration of economic restructuring and its implications for Canadian women leads her to dismiss the so-called 'feminization' thesis which suggests that increased competition and women's historically lower wages will encourage a feminization of labour in the global economy (a substitution of women for men workers). Through an analysis of the statistical trends, Cohen concludes that widespread unemployment, brought about by neo-liberal adjustment policies, has led to a downward pressure on wages that has reinforced gendered labour-market rigidities in Canada. The major change for Canadian women appears to be an increase in non-standard forms of work and a reduction in their labour-force participation rate. She urges that economic adjustment policies include, as a key element, an evaluation of labour impacts along with other macro-economic assessments.

Barbara Evers offers a careful consideration of changes in the demand for labour in the manufacturing sector in Indonesia during the period of stabilization and structural adjustment. Through concrete examples, Evers develops a methodology for evaluating the gender dynamics of macro-economic policy measures. She notes that one cannot predict, prima facie, what the gender implications of adjustment will be, and outlines a number of factors that circumscribe and constrain outcomes: the national economy in a global context; the national economy from the domestic vantage point; industry and sub-sectoral considerations (capital-intensive versus labour-intensive; tradeables versus non-tradeables); the enterprise; regional dynamics of adjustment; the household. A consideration of statistical analysis and data availability issues gives this chapter broader applicability to those wishing to undertake a gender-sensitive evaluation of macro-economic policies.

Nilufer Cagatay also considers the feminization thesis, but in the Turkish context. She argues that an understanding of feminization through flexible labour must start with separating the trends in female employment from the effects of particular macro/industrialization policies. Surveying the segregation of the economy, isolating the urban labour force and zeroing in on manufacturing and home-working, all lead Cagatay to conclude that particular groups of women represent a change in the form of organization of production activities generally dominated by women. The 'alliance' of patriarchal relations that shapes the lives of home-workers and the particular industrialization strategy of the 1980s have created a small female niche of employment that should not lead one to conclude that an economy-wide or urban feminization has taken place.

Antonieta Barrón considers the impact of restructuring and neo-liberal macro-policies on rural women wage earners, specifically those employed in vegetable production in Mexico. She ascertains a trend toward feminization of waged workers that can be attributed to labour shortages rather than low wages per se. Despite women's access to wages that are substantially higher than the national minimum, Barrón points to the contradictory aspects of women's integration into production: wages help to reproduce women and their families, but the conditions under which this reproduction takes place, both in the work place and in the household, are harsh. While internationalization of agricultural production puts demand on increased labour supply, the neo-liberal strategies of the Mexican state have led to cuts in the necessary infrastructural supports required by rural female workers (health, day care). Children's labour is incorporated into the production process whenever a shortage of adult labour occurs. Children are paid below the minimum wage and forgo education in the migratory quest for jobs. In addition, female children often contribute to maintenance and reproduction, and tend the family's plot of land. Barrón is not optimistic about the possibility of state regulation at this conjuncture of economic development.

Haleh Afshar uses case-study research on two countries, Chile and Iran, to advance her argument that state ideologies play an important part in determining policies and selecting national priorities. These, in turn, can yield unexpected costs and benefits for women of differing classes. In the Iranian case, the Islamic fundamentalist ideology of the revolutionary government has imposed unemployment on large numbers of women and reinforced the segregation of the public and the private. Any hopes of an increase in employment in the public sector (in the 'caring' professions), as predicted by some observers, have not been realized. In the Chilean example of market liberalization, Afshar notes that the gendered dimension of the labour market is implicit rather than legally enforced, and results for women have been mixed, with some gains and some losses. Whilst both governments demanded women's confinement to the private sphere, the respective policy outcomes have contradictory implications that can be directly linked to religious ideology. Afshar demonstrates that states can pursue contradictory economic strategies that may not be guided by purely economic criteria or rational decision-making, but also by ideologies of the public/ private boundary and appropriate gender relations.

Swapna Mukhopadhyay's contribution reflects a broader epistemological debate within both economics and feminist theory about the role of social scientists and the formation of concepts and ideas. She challenges the notion that macro-economic concepts are imbued with male bias. Instead, Mukhopadhyay sees the social environment as biased against women, and this in turn is reinforced by policy-makers' lack of gender-disaggregated information, which prevents them from effectively monitoring the impact of policy changes on the public and private spheres. Concepts are circumscribed by the context within which they operate rather than, as Bakker suggests, part of the process of knowledge creation itself. Mukhopadhyay briefly highlights the example of home-working as a distributional scenario resulting from economic-policy changes at the macro-level. Resulting marginalization of female labour from structural adjustment measures points to both the need for policy intervention and the necessity of micro-level studies that complement our understanding of mechanisms at the macro-level.

In summary, this volume contributes to the growing literature on globalization and gender relations. Its focus on macro-economic policy reform reflects a conviction that the direction of aggregate economic development is as profoundly important in shaping the everyday lives of women as are policies directly targeted at women in labour markets. Both sets of policy intervention are of course vital to improving the access of both men and women to resources and decision-making. Yet, macro-economic policies in particular shape and constrain the operation of labour markets through various fiscal, monetary and revenue initiatives. As revealed by the contributors to this volume, the experiences of women and men are frequently fractured and contradictory and reflect tensions between the positions of the North and the South in the globalization process. Overcoming subordination and engendering economic-policy reform will require a commitment to the recognition of the interdependence of the productive and reproductive sectors of the economy, and to broader human development targets that reflect an improved quality of life and democratic empowerment.

Notes

1. By the term 'discourse' I am referring not only to concepts but also to the actual process of knowledge creation that structures how we understand the world. Standard economics presents a discourse that characterizes individual, choosing subjects that are utility maximizers, and integrates the micro-, meso- and macro-levels within this choice-theoretic framework.

2. See Cox (1991) for an extended discussion of national policy constraints in the context of globalization.

3. Some authors have convincingly argued that the structural changes of the 1980s have embedded within them a reprivatization discourse that promotes the reconstitution of the private realm to pre-Keynesian norms (Brodie, forthcoming).

4. It is really men who are commodified, that is, made capable of selling their labour power on the market through the labour done by women in the family; women are decommodified by their very position in the family. As Langan and Ostner have pointed out: 'The role of social rights in decommodification differs according to gender, in general protecting men's position in the labour market while disadvantaging women by restricting their access to certain areas of employment. This process is complex: in some circumstances, as for example in Sweden, social rights may decommodify men while also commodifying women. In contrast to men, women might be commodified as well as decommodified by welfare regimes depending on their relationship to the family' (1991).

5. This cuts across all four of the government spending functions.

References

Addison, Tony and Lionel Demery (1985) *Macro-economic Stabilization, Income Distribution and Poverty: A Preliminary Survey.* Working Paper No. 15, ODI, London.

Afshar, Haleh and Carolyne Dennis (eds) (1992) *Women and Adjustment in the Third World.* Macmillan, Basingstoke.

Applebaum, Eileen (1991) *The Integration of Household Structure and Industrial Structure: An Extension of the Input-Output Model* (mimeo). Wissenschaftszentrum, Berlin.

Appleton, Simon (1991) 'Gender Dimensions of Structural Adjustment: The Role of Economic Theory and Quantitative Analysis'. In *IDS Bulletin,* vol. 22, no. 1, 17–21.

Bakker, Isabella (1988) 'Women's Employment in Comparative Perspective'. In J. Jenson, E. Hagen and C. Reddy (eds), *Feminization of the Labour Force: Paradoxes and Promises.* Polity Press, Cambridge.

——— (1990) 'Pay Equity and Economic Restructuring: The Polarization of Policy?' In J. Fudge and P. McDermott (eds), *Just Wages: A Feminist Assessment of Pay Equity.* University of Toronto Press, Toronto.

Beneria, Lourdes and Shelley Feldman (eds) (1992) *Unequel Burden: Economic Crises, Persistent Poverty, and Women's Work.* Westview Press, Boulder, Co.

Beneria, Lourdes and Martha Roldan (1987) *The Crossroads of Class and Gender*. University of Chicago Press, Chicago and London.

Bowles, Samuel (1991) 'What Markets Can and Cannot Do'. In *Challenge*, vol. 34, no. 4, July/August.

Brodie, Janine (forthcoming) 'The Constitutional Confidence Game: The Economic Union Proposals and the Politics of Restructuring'.

Brown, Claire and Joseph Pechman (eds) (1987) *Gender in the Workplace*. Brookings, Washington DC.

Cagatay, Nilufer and Gunseli Berik (1991) 'Transition to Export-led Growth in Turkey: Is There a Feminisation of Employment?' In *Capital and Class*, vol. 43, no. 2, 153–71.

Cockburn, Cynthia (1983) *Brothers: Male Dominance and Technological Change*. Pluto Press, London.

Collier, Paul (1989) 'Analysis Plan: Role of Women Under Structural Adjustment'. SDA Unit Memo, World Bank, Washington DC.

Commission of the European Communities (1992) *The Position of Women on the Labour Market*. Women of Europe Supplements, no. 36, Brussels.

Commonwealth Secretariat Expert Group on Women and Structural Adjustment (1989) *Engendering Adjustment for the 1990s*. Commonwealth Secretariat, London.

Cornia, Giovanni, Richard Jolly and Frances Stewart (1987) *Adjustment with a Human Face*. Clarendon Press, Oxford.

Cox, Robert (1991) 'The Global Political Economy and Social Choice'. In Daniel Drache and Meric Gertler (eds) *The New Era of Global Competition*. McGill-Queens University Press, Canada.

Crowley, Helen and Susan Himmelweit (1992) *Knowing Women: Feminism and Knowledge*. Polity Press, Cambridge.

Edwards, Meredith (1980) 'Financial Arrangements within Families', Australia: National Women's Advisory Council.

Ekins, Paul and Manfred Max-Neef (1992) *Real-Life Economics: Understanding Wealth Creation*. Routledge, London.

Elson, Diane (1987) *The Impact of Structural Adjustment on Women: Concepts and Issues*. Discussion Papers in Development Studies, DP8801, Manchester.

———— (1991) *Male Bias in the Development Process*. Manchester University Press, Manchester.

———— (1992) *Gender Analysis and Development Economics*. Paper for the ESRC Development Economics Group annual conference, Manchester.

———— (1993) 'Gender-Aware Analysis and Development Economics'. In *Journal of International Development*, vol. 5, no. 2.

Feldman, Shelley (1992) 'Crises, Poverty, and Gender Inequality: Current Themes and Issues'. In Lourdes Beneria and Shelley Feldman (eds) *Unequal Burden: Economic Crises, Persistent Poverty, and Women's Work*. Westview Press, Boulder.

Floro Sagrario, Maria (1991) 'Market Orientation and the Reconstitution of Women's Role in Philippine Agriculture'. In *Review of Radical Political Economy*, vol. 23, nos. 3 and 4.

Folbre, Nancy (1986) 'Cleaning House: New Perspectives on Households and Economic Development'. In *Journal of Development Economics*, vol. 22.

———— (1992) *Rotten Kids, Bad Daddies, and Public Policy*. Paper prepared for presentation at the International Food Policy Research Institute–World Bank Conference on Intrahousehold Resource Allocation, 12–14 February, Washington DC.

Fraser, Nancy (1989) *Unruly Practices: Power, Discourse and Gender in Contemporary Social Theory*. Polity Press, Cambridge.

Freeman, Chris (1992) *Technical Change and Future Trends in the World Economy* (mimeo). Social Policy Research Unit, University of Sussex.

Glyn, Andrew (1992) 'The Costs of Stability: The Advanced Capitalist Countries in the 1980s'. In *New Left Review* 195.

Gordon, Linda (1990) *Women, the State and Welfare*. University of Wisconsin Press, Madison.

Haddad, Lawrence (1991) *Gender and Adjustment: Theory and Evidence to Date*. Paper presented at the Workshop on the Effects of Policies and Programs on Women, International Food Policy Research Institute, Washington DC.

Hodgson, Geoff (1992) 'Rationality and the Influence of Institutions'. In Paul Ekins and Manfred Max-Neef (eds) *Real-Life Economics: Understanding Wealth Creation*. Routledge, London.

Jenson, Jane, Elisabeth Hagen and Ceallaigh Reddy (eds) (1988) *Feminization of the Labour Force: Paradoxes and Promises*. Polity Press, Cambridge.

Joekes, Susan (1988) *Gender and Macro-Economic Policy*. Paper prepared for Association of Women in Development Colloquium on Gender and Development Cooperation, Washington DC.

Kabeer, Naila and Susan Joekes (1991) *IDS Bulletin*, vol. 22, no. 1.

Koopman, Jeanne (1991) 'Neo-classical Household Models and Modes of Household Production: Problems in the Analysis of African Agricultural Households'. In *Review of Radical Political Economy*, vol. 23, nos 3 and 4.

Langan, Mary and Ilona Ostner (1991) 'Gender and Welfare: Towards a Comparative Framework'. Mimeo.

Lewis, Jane and Ilona Ostner (1990) *Gender and the Evolution of European Social Policies*. Paper prepared for the Center for European Studies, Harvard.

MacDonald, Martha and Pat Connelly (1989) 'Class and Gender in Fishing Communities in Nova Scotia'. In *Studies in Political Economy* 30.

Mackintosh, Maureen (1990) 'Abstract Markets and Real Needs'. In Henry Bernstein (ed.) *The Food Question: Profits vs. People?* Monthly Review Press, New York.

Mayatech Corporation (1991) *Gender and Adjustment*. Report prepared for the Office of Women in Development, Bureau for Program and Policy Coordination, US Agency for International Development.

Moser, Caroline (1991) *Urban Poverty and Social Policy in the Context of Adjustment*. Research proposal, Urban Development Division, World Bank, Washington DC.

Moser, Caroline and Peter Sollis (1991) 'A Methodological Framework for Analyzing the Social Costs of Adjustment at the Micro-Level: The Case of Guayaquil, Ecuador'. In *IDS Bulletin*, vol. 22, no. 1.

Mosley, Hugh and Gunther Schmid (1992) *Public Services and Competitiveness*. FS I 92–5. Wissenschaftszentrum, Berlin.

OECD (1985) *OECD Economic Studies*, no. 17, Spring.

———— (1991a) *Shaping Structural Change: The Role of Women*. OECD, Paris.

———— (1991b) 'Controlling Government Spending and Deficits'. In *OECD Economic Studies*, no. 17, Autumn.

———— (1992) *Industrial Policy in OECD Countries*. Annual Review 1992. OECD, Paris.

———— (1993) *Women and Structural Change in the 1990s*. Report by Gunther Schmid. OECD, Paris.

Ostry, Sylvia (1991) 'Beyond the Border: The New International Policy Arena'. In *Strategic Industries in a Global Economy: Policy Issues for the 1990s*. OECD, Paris.

Palmer, Ingrid (1991) *Gender and Population in the Adjustment of African Economies: Planning for Change*. ILO, Geneva.

———— (1992) 'Gender Equity and Economic Efficiency in Adjustment Programmes'. In H. Afshar and C. Dennis (eds) *Women and Adjustment in the Third World*. Macmillan, Basingstoke.

Rubery, Jill (ed.) (1988) *Women and Recession*. Routledge and Kegan Paul, London.

Sen, A.K. (1990) 'Gender and Cooperative Conflicts'. In I. Tinker (ed.) *Persistent Inequalities: Women and World Development*. Oxford University Press, New York.

Sen, Gita (1991) *Macroeconomic Policies and the Informal Sector: A Gender Sensitive Approach*. Working Paper no. 13, Vassar Department of Economics.

Sen, Gita and Caren Grown (1987) *Development, Crises, and Alternative Visions*. Monthly Review, New York.

Soja, Edward (1991) *Postmodern Geographies*. Verso, London.

Standing, Guy (1989) 'Global Feminization Through Flexible Labour'. In *World Development*, vol. 17, no. 7.

Stewart, Frances (1992) 'Can Adjustment Programmes Incorporate the Interests of Women?' in H. Afshar and C. Dennis (eds) *Women and Adjustment in the Third World*. Macmillan, Basingstoke.

Tokman, Victor (1989) 'Policies for a Heterogeneous Informal Sector in Latin America'. In *World Development*, vol. 17, no. 7.

UNDP (1992) *Human Development Report 1992*. United Nations, New York.

UNICEF (1987) *The Invisible Adjustment: Poor Women and the Economic Crisis*. United Nations, Santiago.

Vickers, Jill (1991) 'Bending the Iron Law of Oligarchy: Debates on the Feminization of Political Process in the English Canadian Women's Movement, 1970–1988'. In Jeri Dawn Wine and Janice Ristock (eds) *Women and Social Change: Feminist Activism in Canada*. James Lorimer and Co., Toronto.

Wheelock, Jane (1992) 'The Household in the Total Economy'. In Paul Ekins and Manfred Max-Neef (eds) *Real-Life Economics: Understanding Wealth Creation*. Routledge, London.

Whitehead, Anne (1979) 'Some Preliminary Notes on the Subordination of Women'. In *IDS Bulletin*, vol. 10, no. 3.

Williams, Marjorie (1988) *The Global Economic Crisis, Structural Adjustment and the Fate of Women*. Women's Alternative Economic Summit Draft Paper.

World Development (1989) Special Issue, vol. 17, no. 7.

Young, Kate, Carol Wolkowitz and Roslyn McCullagh (eds) (1981) *Of Marriage and the Market: Women's Subordination in International Perspective*. CSE Books, London.

Table 1.1 Gender Implications of Economic Policy

Type of Policy	Resulting Gender Asymmetries
(A) Macro-economic Policies	
The macro-economy reflects the aggregate or overall supply and demand of goods and services, the level of prices and employment, the balance of trade in goods and services and financial flows with the rest of the world.	Macro-economic conditions have a significant and distinctive impact on women's lives often greater than WID or equal-opportunities projects because they reflect the parameters of 'the possible' in economic terms.
1. Revenue-raising measures	
Direct (income taxes) and indirect (consumption, VAT taxes)	Direct taxes have a greater incidence among men because of their access to earnings; indirect consumption taxes are said to have a greater impact on women as managers of the household consumption budget.
	Wealth taxes between and within families rest largely on public policy assumptions about the family and property. Palmer's 'reproduction labour tax' falls disproportionately on women and leads to gender-based distortions in resources and labour-market mobility.
2. Government expenditures	
Four major government spending functions are usually isolated: (i) 'pure' public goods provision (defence, government administrative services); (ii) merit goods (education, health, housing); (iii) income maintenance and other transfers; and (iv) general economic services.

Examples:
(a) public-sector employment (spans all four areas of government expenditure);
(b) capital expenditures (economic services): | (a) Women in public-sector employment generally face better terms and conditions of work and remuneration than in the private sector, hence macro policy initiatives that lead to cuts in public-sector employment and pay are particularly negative for the labour-market status and opportunities of women; cuts can also have spill-over effects in terms of shifting work to women in the private sphere (e.g., care of the sick and elderly).
(b) Capital expenditures and cuts have a disproportionate effect on men given their generally above-average participation in these sectors.
(c) Subsidies can have a differential impact on the sexes depending on what prices and goods are controlled (e.g., food and fuel) and which industries retain employment, whether subsidies are complementary or compensatory, and whether direct or indirect.
(d) Service delivery in health, education and training has been shown to have a male bias in client benefit, although cutbacks in child care, etc., transfer costs to women, and cuts in goods and services subsidized by the government (electricity, public transport, basic |

(c) subsidies (economic services);

(d) service delivery and goods provision (merit goods);

(e) transfers (income maintenance and other transfers).

food-stuffs) increase pressures on those who administer the household on a daily basis.

(e) The extent to which individual economic security depends on transfers (for example, old-age benefits versus private pensions) needs to be distinguished along gender lines – there are inequities in transfers received, e.g. unemployment benefits.

3. Monetary and exchange-rate policies

Monetary policy is how government influences the rate of interest in order to regulate the level of investment, output, employment and other macro-economic outcomes.

Monetary policy often targets exchange rates and is used by governments to promote (by reducing the value of the currency) or discourage (by pushing up the value of the currency) exports and hence, influence the level and type of domestic production activity and employment.

Uncovering the gender dimensions of interest rate targets involves an examination of the immediate effects of interest rates on different types of economic activities plus a careful consideration of the secondary consequences due to changes in the cost of living; it is with this latter impact that non-production activity needs to be surveyed, as cost-cutting is often absorbed by women's increased labour in the household and in the care-giving sector; studies have also shown a disproportionate cut in food consumption by women and young girls in the case of household budget cuts (this has long-term health effects).

Asymmetrical ability in mobility and switching from non-tradeables to tradeables in the case of SAP.

High-interest-rate policies may have asymmetrical outcomes in terms of unemployment rates and pressures to reduce government deficits.

(B) Market Regulations

Reflect the attempt by governments to set the operating parameters in the land, labour, financial and product markets.

1. Labour markets

These are regulated by public-sector wage policy (e.g., equal pay for work of equal value), minimum wage laws for the public and private sectors, conditions for recognizing labour organizations, leave, retirement, etc.

The most obvious examples are the setting of differential wage levels by sex, 'protective' legislation which may limit women's access to paid employment; and this can put pressure on the reserve price of female labour in the informal sector.

Gender-segmented labour markets determine the nature and quality of employment; this in turn affects job security, entitlements, rewards.

2. Land markets

These are regulated through the bureaucratization of title and registration, minimum and maximum size restrictions.

These may be influenced by gender-based distortions in inheritance, property rights laws, etc.

3. Financial markets

These are regulated via restrictions on the establishment, operation and lending conditions set by financial institutions and by interest-rate provisions; banks have fixed-deposit ratios and are limited in their access to foreign markets.

These may reflect the lesser property rights for women enshrined in social policies through requirements for collateral and/or male signatories in the case of loans.

Women's lesser claim to earnings which are loan collateral may dispose banks against women.

Parallel problems exist in agricultural credit (e.g., Africa and land title formalization).

4. Product markets

These are frequently subject to direct price controls by governments on essential commodities, or ceilings can be set on price increases

These may magnify women's economic disadvantages as their access to price-controlled goods can be penalized in two ways: (i) they may have less claims within households to goods acquired for household consumption (e.g., under-feeding of female children); (ii) women are overrepresented among the poorest households in many countries.

(C) Social Policies

Legal instruments which set the conditions and govern the terms of marriage and family formation, divorce and child custody, inheritance, property rights, rights outside and within marriage, e.g., assault.

Instruments are strongly asymmetrical by sex, e.g., marital violence.

Lesser property rights reinforce women's lesser claim to income from labour and weaken their bargaining position in the household and within marriage.

The universality of marriage and the custom of cutting ties with the woman's natal family have important economic consequences for their lifetime earning capacity, access to education and training.

Women bear a disproportionate portion of the cost of reproduction.

Sources: Compiled by the author; some references are from Joekes, 1988, and Elson, 1991.

PART I

Conceptual Silences and New Research Strategies

2

Micro, Meso, Macro:
Gender and Economic Analysis in
the Context of Policy Reform
Diane Elson

Economists traditionally divide economics into a supply side and a demand side, and look at the functioning of economies at the micro-level of supply and demand interactions between individual economic agents, and at the macro-level of aggregate supply and demand. More recently, some economists have explicitly introduced into the analysis a third level, the meso, between the macro and the micro. Meso analysis concerns itself with the structures that mediate between individuals and the economy considered as a whole, by providing economic signals, costs and benefits, and typically focuses on markets, private-sector firms and public-sector services.

This chapter examines how concepts of the micro, the macro and the meso are used by orthodox and critical economists in discussions of economic policy reform; and the extent to which these concepts recognize gender. We also consider some feminist strategies for enabling economic analysis at these three levels to contribute towards the empowerment of women, rather than the perpetuation of their subordination.

The advocacy of economic policy reform: micro, macro and meso in the neo-classical perspective

The dominant analysis of economic policy reform is based on neo-classical economics. From this perspective there is no inherent reason why an economy based on voluntary contracts between individuals should experience any persistent problems. Such an economy should be self-regulating, in the sense that supply and demand are quickly brought into equality at micro- and macro-levels through the mediating structure of the market mechanism (that is, the economy tends towards general equilibrium). Such an economy should also be efficient, in the specific sense that it results in outcomes where no one can be made better off without someone else being made worse off (that is, the economy tends towards Pareto optimality).[1] Finally, the economy should also experience dynamic development, as voluntary contracts between individuals mediated by the market mechanism supposedly encourage initiative and innovation, and the best use of scarce resources.

In the neo-classical paradigm, micro-, meso- and macro-levels are fully integrated, and simply represent pictures of the economy at varying levels of detail. The macro-level looks at the economy in terms of total marketed output (domestic private-sector and public-sector production plus imports) and total expenditure (consumption plus private investment plus government expenditure plus exports). These aggregates are understood as a coherent result of the activities of millions of individuals (micro-level) integrated by the institutions of the meso-level. The private-sector institutions operating at the meso-level, the institutions of the market mechanism and the firm, are understood as the outcome of voluntary contracts by individuals who wish to create institutions to economize on the costs of conducting transactions (see Hodgson, 1988 for a critical explanation). What is economically rational at the individual level also appears to be economically rational at the level of society as a whole.

If things are not working out like this, and there are problems of budget and balance-of-payments deficits, inflation and unemployment, then the main problem is argued to lie in the wrong sort of public policies at macro- and meso-levels. Public policy is conceptualized as an intervention in the economy from the outside, an intervention made not by individuals but by the state, acting not via voluntary contracts but by legislative commands. The wrong sort of public policy leads to imbalances at the macro-level between aggregate supply and demand brought about by the wrong sort of fiscal and monetary policy; by giving individuals the wrong sort of economic signals at the meso-level it leads to imbalances at the micro-level between supply and demand for particular goods and services. This creates inefficiency and undermines dynamic development. The wrong sort of public policy also prevents an economy being able to adapt easily to change, particularly to 'external shocks' coming from the international economy, such as rises in interest rates, falls in the terms of trade, and falls in inflows of finance.

Changes therefore need to be made in state intervention at macro- and meso-levels. Typically, the reforms recommended include cutbacks in aggregate public expenditure and the money supply, to reduce aggregate demand and a whole series of changes at the meso-level, to remove so-called 'distortions' in the economic signals transmitted to individuals and the economic costs and benefits they enjoy. These will include changes in prices (for instance via devaluation, trade liberalization, and withdrawal of subsidies) and in infrastructural services (such as transport, training, education and health services).

The state tends to be conceptualized as absent from the micro-level, which is seen as a private sphere of economic individuals. However, the very ability of a person to function as an economic individual – that is, an individual able to enter into voluntary contracts to exchange goods and services – is constituted by the state. A gender-aware perspective is much more likely to recognize this, because it will be concerned with economic woman as well as economic man. The ability of women to enter into economic contracts is constrained by the way that state legislation typically construes women as less than full citizens. A key example of this in the context of economic policy reform in many developing countries is the way in which the ability of women to enter into credit contracts is constrained by women's lack of rights to family assets. All too often, women cannot sign contracts in their own right and require a male guarantor (father, brother, husband). There is no such thing as a purely private level of the economy.

A related key issue in economic policy reform, but one which is often neglected, is how the reforms change the rights enjoyed by individuals. Where this *is* considered, it tends to be in terms of an enhancement of individual property rights brought about by privatization. But privatization typically also reduces individual social rights of employees, and certainly reduces the collective rights of the citizens over economic assets. Individual social rights can also be reduced in the course of economic policy reform by shifts of employment from the 'formal' to the 'informal' sector; by erosion of customary use rights to land by commercialization of land; and by direct legislative change to withdraw or restructure state-provided services and benefits and to abolish employee rights, such as minimum-wage legislation and the right to strike (see Standing, 1989, and Elson, 1991 for a discussion of this in relation to labour markets). Removal of rights is very often undertaken in the name of removing 'distortions' from markets. However, unequal distribution of wealth and income is not considered a 'distortion', and reduction of the property rights of the rich and powerful does not tend to feature on the current agendas of economic policy reform.[2] Rather, it is the poor and weak who are much more likely to find that their social rights are regarded as 'distortions'.

The family,[3] one might think, should logically be regarded as belonging to the meso-level – it is, after all, a social institution that brings people together and mediates between them. In economic analysis, however, the family is usually assigned to the *micro*-level. Indeed, neoclassical analysis treats the family as if it were an individual: in technical terms it is assumed that the family has a joint utility function, and that an altruistic head of household makes decisions on behalf of the family that maximize the joint activity of its members. This means that, provided the 'right' economic signals reach a family via state agencies, markets and firms, the division of labour and distribution of income within a family is bound to be 'optimal', simply reflecting the different tastes and skills of family members. (This is known in the literature as the 'new household economics'; for critical discussion, see Evans, 1989, and Folbre, 1986.)

At the micro-level, the neo-classical approach can accommodate gender difference, and even some degree of gender inequality. Economic agents can easily be characterized as 'male' or 'female', in a way that macro-economic aggregates cannot. But gender differentiation must be conceptualized as a matter of differences in the preferences and resource endowments (including skills) of individuals, if the fundamental neo-classical characterization of human beings as utility maximizers with well-defined choice sets and preference orderings is to be preserved. The key problem for women is then judged to be discrimination against them, in a variety of transactions, by other economic agents. But discrimination is judged to be in itself generally commercially irrational, leading to lower monetary returns for the discriminating agent. Thus commercialization is seen as generally acting in ways advantageous to women by undermining prejudice.[4] From this point of view, economic policy reforms which strengthen commercialization and the profit motive are seen as likely to work to women's advantage.

At the meso- and macro-levels, neo-classical analysis excludes gender. Mediating structures and monetary aggregates cannot be identified as 'male' or 'female', and so gender analysis is seen as out of place. Indeed, meso institutions and macro-policy instruments tend to be seen as 'gender neutral' (see also Elson, 1991). If these institutions and instruments operate in ways that are detrimental to women, then this is fundamentally due to the characteristics of individuals at the micro-level, and in particular to prejudice against women. The appropriate policy response is equal-opportunities legislation, education to combat prejudice, and 'safety nets' for women denied gainful employment – not a restructuring of meso institutions and a rethinking of macro-policy reforms. Gender has a place only at the micro-level, in the analysis of the responses of individuals to the reforms.

The critique of economic policy reform: micro, macro and meso in the perspectives of critical economics

There is a variety of economic analyses critical of current forms of economic policy reform, drawing on Keynesian, Kaleckian, structuralist and Marxist perspectives. Critical perspectives stress that what is rational for the individual economic agent is not necessarily rational for the system as a whole. The macro-level of the economy has a life of its own and is not simply an aggregation which synthesizes the preferences and endowments of the individuals who make up the economy. The reason it has a life of its own is that money and the market mechanism do not simply integrate the actions of many individuals, in the way that general equilibrium theory supposes. Money and the market mechanism also disintegrate, fragment and segment individual actions. In particular, there is no guarantee that supply and demand for goods will be brought into line by price changes, with money acting simply as a medium of exchange. If agents think prices will change in the future, it makes sense for them to hold on to money itself, rather than use it to buy something right now (see Bhaduri, 1986 for further explanation).

Once this is taken into account, the economy can be seen as something with the potential to generate its own problems, such as unemployment, inflation, debt, and declining productivity. Economic crisis is not just the result of the wrong policies and 'external shocks'. Indeed, the 'external shocks' themselves can be seen as resulting from inherent dysfunctions of the international economy. A corollary of this is that the macro-level should not just be analysed on a country-by-country basis. It should be analysed at a global, as well as a national level. Policy reform should extend to the international system of trade and payments (see Helleiner, 1992).

Critical perspectives also challenge the idea that the institutions of the firm and the market mechanism can simply be derived from the utility-maximizing decisions of individuals (argued in depth by Hodgson, 1988). One strand of analysis emphasizes that these institutions embody co-operative conflicts, that is, situations in which individuals do stand to make gains from co-operating (for example, producing something together on the basis of a wage contract) but have different and conflicting interests in the distribution of the benefits (see also Drèze and Sen, 1989). Partly as a way of coping with this, meso-institutions embody social norms and networks which themselves shape the behaviour of individuals and the ideas they have about what it is appropriate to want and to do. Without such social norms market economies could not function, because voluntary contracts between individuals are always incomplete. This is because life is radically uncertain, and try as we might to cover all contingencies, the unexpected is always liable to crop up. The outcome will depend on the degree to which people feel bound to act in certain ways even though there is not a clause in the contract to cover it, on what labour market analysts call 'custom and practice', on shared general understandings and mutual trust (see Hodgson, 1988).

Similar sorts of analysis have also been extended to the family, which has been seen as a social institution that is an area of co-operative conflict in which behaviour is constrained by social norms. In the work of some economists the analysis also extends to calling into question the fundamental characterization of human beings as economic agents. It may be argued that the experience of subordination makes people less likely to have a well-defined preference function. The experience of subordination inclines people to shape their preferences to what is available, rather than reach out for what they want. Social norms constrain the choices that people make about the division of labour in the family. A notable example of this type of analysis of the family may be found in Sen, 1990.

This perspective easily lends itself to an analysis of gender inequality at the micro-level that is much more critical than that offered by the neo-classical paradigm. Rather than the gender division of labour and income in the family being seen as the optimal outcome of free choices, it may be seen as the profoundly unequal accommodation reached between individuals who occupy very different social positions with very different degrees of social power. Individuals may be conceptualized not just as biologically male and female but as socially gendered (as in Sen, 1990). Most critical economics, however, shares with neo-classical economics a lack of gender analysis at the meso- and macro-levels. Although individuals are conceptualized as gendered in the critical economics of the family, markets and firms are not generally conceptualized as gendered in a comparable way, though they may operate in ways that are particularly constraining and disadvantageous to women. At the macro-level, gender is absent altogether: the discourse is all about monetary aggregates. Many critical economists are puzzled about how gender analysis can be introduced at a level of economic analysis which is completely impersonal. However, feminist critical economics has begun to show us how we can demonstrate that not only is the personal political, the impersonal is political too!

Feminist critical economics and the critique of economic policy reform

Feminist critical economics[5] argues that the operation of economic reform at micro-, meso- and macro-levels is male-biased, serving to perpetuate women's relative disadvantage, even though the forms of that disadvantage vary between different groups of women and are disrupted and change in the course of policy reform. Most economic theory, whether orthodox or critical, is also male-biased, even though it appears to be gender-neutral. The male bias arises because theory fails to take adequate account of the inequality between women as a gender and men as a gender. Neo-classical economics is fundamentally disabled from doing this because of its 'choice-theoretic' framework of analysis. Critical economics opens up the possibility of theory which is not male-biased, and of economic policy reforms which are not male-biased, because it does not regard micro-, meso- and macro-levels of the economy as integrated and regulated by a choice-theoretic logic. Feminist critical economics starts from these possibilities.[6]

Most feminist critical work to date has concentrated on the micro-level. The feminist critique of economic policy reform has concentrated on investigating the impact of economic policy reform at the level of the family and the individual, utilizing a bargaining-based critical theory of the family, and arguing that the burdens placed on poor rural and poor urban women are incommensurate with any benefits they may possibly obtain (see, for example, Beneria and Feldman, 1992).

It is necessary to go beyond this and to analyse how male bias is constituted at the meso- and macro-levels, at the level of mediating institutions and monetary aggregates. One way of doing this is to investigate how social institutions and monetary relationships which are not themselves intrinsically gendered nevertheless become bearers of gender.[7] The family is an intrinsically gendered institution, in that the conjugal relation that constitutes it is gender ascriptive. Marriage is a social relation between a person of the male and a person of the female gender. Kin relations are gender ascriptive – the discourse of kin indicates the gender of the persons referred to (sister, brother, nephew, niece, grandmother, grandfather).

Commercial relations between buyer and seller, and employer and employee, are not intrinsically gendered in this way. Neither are the relations between users and providers of public services. But although they are not gender ascriptive, these relations are bearers of gender, in the sense that they are permeated through and through by gender in their institutional structure. As one study of Brazilian factories concluded, 'the supposedly objective economic laws of market competition work through and within "gendered structures"' (Humphrey, 1985: 219).

At the meso-level, the operation of markets, firms, and public-sector agencies is gendered via the social norms and networks which are functional to the smooth operation of those institutions. Social cohesion between men is enhanced by the exclusion of women. Social discipline in hierarchical organizations is enhanced by the systematic subordination of women. Critical institutional economics has tended to stress the social benefits of customs which fill the gaps in incomplete contracts, in order to stress that economics cannot be understood simply in terms of contracts and cash nexuses. But although such customs may be beneficial in allowing economies to continue to function, the benefits tend to be very unequally distributed. Shared social understandings and mutual trust tend to be expressions of the hegemony of the powerful. Thus, although women may formally be able to participate in markets, they tend to find themselves excluded from the traditional business–social networks, where vital exchanges of information occur and 'goodwill' is built up.[8] Similarly, although women may formally be able to participate in paid employment in the private sector, they tend to find themselves excluded from the teams of skilled and professional workers who obtain the higher incomes.[9]

Economic policy reform often involves the emergence of new meso-level institutions. Rolling back the state means the emergence of new markets and new firms. Reforming public-sector services means the emergence of new types of public-sector agency. Unless explicit thought is given to the design of these new institutions, they will tend to instigate new instances of male bias.[10] Women will be excluded from or disadvantaged in their operations. The shared social understandings on which they rest will be expressive of male hegemony. Even though the policy reforms may not be male-biased by design, they will be male-biased by omission.

At the meso-level, therefore, we can introduce gender analysis via an examination of how the social norms and networks which are needed for the successful operation of both commercial and public-service institutions are bearers of gender.

At the macro-level the crucial thing to consider is the role of money. Money mobilizes human effort, via prices and wages; and the output of effort that it mobilizes gets counted in the gross national product, and in other monetary aggregates such as savings, investment, public expenditure, public revenue, imports and exports. But money's mobilizing power is incomplete. It is not able to mobilize directly all the resources that go into reproducing and maintaining the capacity for effort (labour-power) in any economy which is based on wage labour rather than slave labour. The ability of money to mobilize labour power for 'productive work' depends on the operation of some non-monetary set of social relations to mobilize labour power for 'reproductive work'. These non-monetary social relations are subordinate to money in the sense that they cannot function and sustain themselves without an input of money; and they are reshaped in response to the power of money. Nevertheless, neither can the monetary economy sustain itself without an input of unpaid labour, an input shaped by the structure of gender relations. Male bias in gender relations means that the burdens of 'reproductive work' fall mainly on women. There is an interdependence between the economy of monetized production and the non-monetized 'reproductive' economy. One implication of this 'incompleteness' of monetary relations is that money and all its forms (prices, wages, rates of interest, and so on) become 'bearers of gender', expressing male bias both in quantitative terms (as in the differential between male and female wages) and in qualitative terms (as in the difference between paid work which is recognized as productive and unpaid work which is not). Money is not gender-neutral. Women's access to money is structured by gender relations. Such access tends to disrupt non-monetized gender relations, but it results in new forms of gender relations, in which male bias is expressed in monetary form.

The interdependence between the economy of monetized production and the non-monetized economy of 'reproductive work' is a delicate balance, constrained by the fact that basic needs must be met to sustain human beings and human communities, and that monetized production is subject to inherent dislocations and crises. History shows that this interdependence in market economies cannot be successfully regulated by individual contract and monetary relations. It has always required the mediation of the organizations of the state and the community, the provision of public services and community mutual aid, to avoid destitution and social breakdown, and to enhance human development in ways that promote increases in productivity in the monetized economy. It has always required ways of transferring resources that do not entail buying and selling, but operate through taxes and subsidies, gifts and grants.

A feminist critique of economic policy reform at the macro-level can be developed in terms of an analysis of how economic policy reform treats the interdependence between the 'productive economy' and the 'reproductive economy', between making a profit and meeting needs, between covering costs and sustaining human beings. Overwhelmingly, the design of economic policy reform focuses on the 'productive economy'. Macro-policy is generally designed to bring the *level* of aggregate monetized demand in line with the level of aggregate monetized supply, and to change the *structure* of monetized demand and supply so as to favour the production of goods which are internationally tradeable (tradeables) as compared with those that are only domestically tradeable, or which are supplied without charge by the public sector though their production is monetized through the public-sector budget (non-tradeables).

Macro-policy generally takes the 'reproductive economy' for granted, assuming it can continue to function adequately no matter how its relation to the 'productive economy' is disrupted. Current forms of economic policy reform that emphasize rolling back the state and liberating market forces give scant consideration to how this will impact on the 'reproductive economy'. There tends to be an implicit assumption that the 'reproductive economy' can accommodate itself to whatever changes macro-policy introduces, especially to withdrawals of public services and subsidies and declines in public-sector employment and to rises in prices and taxes. Since it is women who undertake most of the work in the 'reproductive economy', and in the organization of community mutual aid, this is equivalent to assuming that there is an unlimited supply of unpaid female labour, able to compensate for any adverse changes resulting from macro-economic policy, so as to continue to meet the basic needs of their families and communities and sustain them as social organizations.

This is the point at which macro-economics is male-biased. It is not that macro-policy reforms are deliberately designed to favour men. Nor is the key issue that male-biased social traditions prevent women from taking advantage of macro-policy reforms that could work in their favour. The key issue is that macro-economics has a one-sided view of the macro-economy: it considers only the monetary aggregates of the 'productive economy'. It ignores the human resource aggregates of the 'reproductive economy', the indicators of population, health, nutrition, education, skills. This one-sided view of the macro-economy is a male-biased view, because the sexual division of labour means that women are largely responsible for the 'reproductive economy' as well as contributing a great deal of effort to the 'productive economy'.[11] This male bias cannot, however, simply be changed by theoretical analysis and research. It requires changes in the way that national and international economies function, so that human development can take priority – a point made in UNDP, 1990. For this to happen, it is not enough to introduce targeted poverty-alleviation programmes ('safety nets'). Rather than bind the wounds after they have been inflicted, it is better not to inflict the wounds in the first place.

Conclusions

One way forward would be to campaign in order that all programmes for macro-economic policy reform include not only targets for monetary aggregates and policy instruments for achieving them but also targets for human development aggregates and policy instruments for delivering them. The relation between the policy instruments and the targets should be analysed in gender-disaggregated terms that recognize inputs of unpaid labour as well as paid labour.[12] We need to ask what kinds of institutions will mediate between changes in fiscal and monetary policy and exchange-rate policy and individuals. What benefits and what costs are different groups of women and men expected to expe-

experience? Has the interdependence between the 'productive economy' and the 'reproductive economy' been taken into account? For instance, has the programme of expenditure cuts been designed in a way that will sustain or undermine the ability of women to respond to new price incentives in agriculture and job opportunities in export-oriented manufacturing, without jeopardizing human development targets?[13]

The integration of human development targets into macro-economic policy reform programmes will also facilitate a view of human beings as ends, not just means, as persons with social rights, not factors of production with prices. Programmes for economic policy reform should be required to specify whose rights (distinguishing rights of men and of women) will be changed, and how. This way of introducing gender-awareness into the design of economic policy reforms is likely to benefit some men as well as women in so far as it introduces consideration of needs and rights into the process of reform alongside dollars and deficits. It combats a male bias in policy reforms which is far from being deliberately introduced by those who design reforms, but which is the result of oversights and omissions facilitated by a one-sided concern with monetary variables. It emphasizes that the key issue we need to address in attempts to engender macro-economic policy reform is not pre-existing customs and traditions which discriminate against women, but one-sided emphasis by reformers on paid work in the 'productive economy', and a neglect of unpaid work in the 'reproductive economy'.

Notes

1. This does *not* necessarily mean a situation where everyone's basic needs are satisfied. Pareto optimality is consistent with a very unequal, as well as a very equal, distribution of income.

2. Land reform is rarely included, even though there are strong reasons to suppose land reform would in many cases improve the efficiency of resource use.

3. I shall use the terms 'family' and 'household' in the rather unquestioning way that economists do. For discussion on the complexities of these social groupings and the problems of where to draw bounds, see *IDS Bulletin,* 1991.

4. Occasionally arguments are presented to suggest that discrimination may be 'rational' and will persist. See, for instance, Birdsall and Sabot, 1991: 10–11.

5. Feminist economics is only just beginning to define itself and make its presence felt in economics as a discipline. Some of the work of those who define themselves as feminist economists draws on the mainstream neo-classical paradigm; other feminist economists draw on a variety of critical approaches, a notable example being Folbre (forthcoming).

6. These issues are explored at greater length in Elson, 1993b (forthcoming) and Elson, 1993a (mimeo).

7. The distinction between social relations which are intrinsically gendered ('gender ascriptive') and those which are not, but which are nevertheless bearers of gender, is due to Whitehead, 1979.

8. As was found by a study of women entrepreneurs in Kenya, Ghana, Jamaica and the Solomon Islands (Commonwealth Secretariat, 1990).

9. This is established in fascinating detail in a study of technical workers in Britain by Cockburn, 1985.

10. For discussion of male bias in state agencies, see Agarwal, 1988.

11. The functioning of the 'reproductive economy' does, of course, require inputs of cash and public services. Indeed, these are vital in improving productivity in the development of human capacities.

12. This requirement goes beyond the prescriptions of the *Human Development Report* (1990), which surprisingly fails to recognize the vital role of *unpaid* labour as a producer of human capacities and one-sidedly emphasizes public-sector services.

13. A study of economic policy reform in Zambia found that cutbacks in health expenditure were hampering women farmers, who were having to spend more time looking after sick relatives, and less time farming (Evans and Young, 1988).

References

Agarwal, B. (ed.) (1988) *Structures of Patriarchy.* Zed Books, London.

Beneria, L. and S. Feldman (eds) (1992) *Economic Crises, Persistent Poverty and Women's Work.* Westview Press, Boulder, Co.

Bhaduri, A. (1986) *Macroeconomics: The Dynamics of Commodity Production.* Macmillan, Basingstoke.

Birdsall, N. and R. Sabot (eds) (1991) *Unfair Advantage: Labour Market Discrimination in Developing Countries.* World Bank, Washington DC.

Cockburn, S. (1985) *Machinery of Dominance: Women, Men and Technical Know-How.* Pluto Press, London.

Commonwealth Secretariat (1990) *Women in Export Development.* Commonwealth Secretariat, London.

Drèze, J. and A.K. Sen (1989) *Hunger and Public Action.* Oxford University Press, Oxford.

Elson, D. (1991) 'Appraising Recent Developments in the World Market for Nimble Fingers: Accumulation, Regulation, Organisation'. Paper presented at Workshop on Women Organising in the Process of Industrialisation, Institute of Social Studies, The Hague.

———— (1993a) 'Feminist Approaches to Development Economics' (mimeo). Department of Economics, University of Manchester.

———— (1993b) 'Gender-Aware Analysis and Development Economics'. In *Journal of International Development,* vol. 5, no. 2.

Evans, A. (1989) *Gender Issues in Rural Household Economics,* Institute of Development Studies Discussion Paper No. 254.

Evans, A. and K. Young (1988) 'Gender Issues in Household Labour Allocation: The Case of Northern Province, Zambia', ODA ESCOR Research Report. Overseas Development Agency, London.

Folbre, N. (1986) 'Hearts and Spades: Paradigms of Household Economics'. In *World Development*, vol. 14, no. 2.

―――― (forthcoming) *The Logic of Patriarchal Capitalism*. Routledge, London.

Helleiner, G.K. (1992) 'The IMF, the World Bank and Africa's Adjustment and External Debt Problems: An Unofficial View'. In *World Development*, vol. 20, no. 6, 779–92.

Hodgson, G. (1988) *Economics and Institutions*. Polity Press, Cambridge.

Humphrey, J. (1985) 'Gender, Pay and Skill: Manual Workers in Brazilian Industry'. In H. Afshar (ed.) *Women, Work and Ideology in the Third World*. Tavistock, London.

IDS Bulletin (1991) Special Issue: 'Researching the Household: Methodological and Empirical Issues', vol. 22, no. 1.

Sen, A.K. (1990) 'Gender and Co-operative Conflicts'. In I. Tinker (ed.) *Persistent Inequalities – Women and World Development*. Oxford University Press, Oxford.

Standing, G. (1989) 'Global Feminisation through Flexible Labour'. In *World Development*, vol. 17, no. 7, 1077–95.

UNDP (1990) *Human Development Report*. Oxford University Press, Oxford.

Whitehead, A. (1979) 'Some Preliminary Notes on the Subordination of Women'. In *IDS Bulletin*, vol. 10, no. 3.

3

Shifting the Boundaries:
Gender and the Politics of Restructuring
Janine Brodie

Although the discourse about global restructuring is invariably cast in gender-neutral terms, gender-sensitive analyses have increasingly demonstrated that women, in both First and Third World countries, are bearing the burden of economic adjustment. Gender-sensitive research is a first and necessary step in an examination of gender and restructuring. But, in this chapter, I argue that it fails to theorize adequately both the multiple dimensions of the process and the role of the state in constituting and reconstituting gender relations during periods of profound structural change. The gendered dimensions of restructuring extend far beyond the economic. Instead, the current round of restructuring entails a fundamental redrawing of the familiar boundaries between the international and national, the state and the economy, and the so-called 'public' and 'private'. This realignment, in turn, undermines both the assumptions and sites of contemporary feminist politics and invites new strategic thinking about the boundaries of the political.

During the past two decades the international political economy has been marked by uncertainty and structural changes which have eroded the governing assumptions of post-World War II nation-states. For most of this century, nation-states acted to promote domestic welfare and to protect national economies from disruptive international forces. Nation-states are now abandoning these priorities and transforming domestic economies to correspond to 'perceived exigencies' of the new international political economy (Cox, 1991: 337). Since the 1970s, pronounced structural shifts, such as the increasing centralization and concentration of capital, the formation of larger markets, the globalization of productive and finance capital, an accelerated geographic mobility of industry, and a new international division of labour, have forced nation-states to search for a new logic of development and complementary political forms (Soja, 1989: 159).

Elements of this new logic were first directly imposed on debt-ridden developing countries by multilateral institutions such as the

International Monetary Fund (IMF) and the World Bank in the form of structural adjustment policies (SAP). These policies forced 'stabilization' through the reduction of debt and government spending and 'adjustment' through deregulation of industry and the expansion of international trade. In the developed world, the influence of the IMF and World Bank has been less direct and the process is more often termed 'economic restructuring' than 'structural adjustment' (Harder, 1992: 7). Nonetheless, the demands on all states are roughly equivalent: maximize exports, reduce social spending, end state economic regulation; and enhance the power of private capital to reorganize national economies as parts of transnational economic networks (Friedman, 1991: 35). The current period, then, entails a period of global and national restructuring. As Soja explains, restructuring 'conveys the notion of a "brake", if not a break, in secular trends, and a shift toward a significantly different order and configuration of social, economic, and political life. It thus evokes a sequential combination of falling apart and building up again, deconstruction and attempted reconstitution' (Soja, 1989: 159).

The origins, multidimensionality and consequences of the current round of restructuring have been central to the work of the French Regulation School, which argues that Western economies are rapidly transforming in response to a crisis in productivity and globalization, passing from the familiar Fordist past to the unknowns of a post-Fordist future. Examining the post-World War II period, these theorists argue that a national political economy, at any conjuncture, can best be viewed as a 'social mould' comprised of three levels of independent but interlocking sets of relations. There is a regime of accumulation, which is a long-term stabilization of a logic of accumulation; a mode of regulation, which is comprised of institutional forms and social procedures that coerce and encourage individuals and groups to act in ways consistent with the logic of the regime of accumulation; and legitimization mechanisms, which help reproduce the system by engendering particular norms of behaviour and representations of reality (see Lipietz, 1987: ch. 1, and 1988; Clarkson, 1991).

According to the regulation theorists, postwar capitalism in developed countries was reproduced under a Fordist mode of regulation. National governments took an active role in managing national economies through Keynesian demand-management techniques; the labour process was organized around the assembly line and mass production; and redistribution was accomplished through social welfare spending and collective bargaining. It is precisely this mode of regulation that has been eroded by the combined front of globalization and its discursive representations in neo-classical economics and neo-conservative politics.

The neo-conservative discourse about the new mode of regulation is cast in terms of inescapable necessity, a neo-Darwinian survival-of-the-fittest which allows no place for politics, compensatory justice, or political agency. It begins with a declaration of profound change and crisis. National governments have lost their ability to regulate national economies because production is now international. The requisites of globalization demand that states and societies adjust to compete on the world market. This adjustment, so the argument goes, necessarily requires a mode of regulation that will enable states to compete successfully for a highly fluid international capital. In order to compete, national econo-mies must become efficient, which means reducing fiscal and regulatory burdens on industry and lowering expectations about the role of the state both in terms of protecting national economies from global pres-sures and providing social welfare. It means decentring and displacing the Keynesian state and pre-empting democratic struggle and political agency with the dictates of the market. In other words, this discourse recommends the shrinkage of the public and political spaces of Fordism and the simultaneous expansion and 're-privatization' of the economy, the community and the home (see Brodie, forthcoming). It recommends a fundamental reordering of the mode of regulation and a new defini-tion of the public good, but is silent about the gendered underpinnings of this shift.

Phallocentric restructuring

Feminist academics have become increasingly sensitive to the role that discourse and representation play in the subordination of women. A discourse can be judged as sexist when women are either ignored or debased, and patriarchal when it assumes and inscribes a sexual division of labour into a representation, thereby denying women and men the same access to self-determination. Finally, and most insidiously, a dis-course is phallocentric when it represents highly gendered social agents or processes in terms of universals and genderless abstracts such as 'worker', 'entrepreneur', 'efficiency' and 'competition' (Grosz, 1990: 149–51). Phallocentric discourses challenge us to reveal how the supposedly neutral and universal are, in fact, inherently gendered, that is, specific representations of the male experience. Put differently, the first and necessary step in a feminist analysis of restructuring is to understand how the dominant discourse of globalization conceals and excludes gender-specific consequences.

Feminist analyses of restructuring have tended to follow two inter-related strategies. The first has been to demonstrate how neo-classical economic theory and globalization discourse, in particular, contain phallocentric and patriarchal assumptions that misrepresent and conceal women's experience. The second has been to apply 'gender-sensitive' assumptions and methods in order to demonstrate empirically the gendered foundations of restructuring. Later in this chapter I shall argue that these approaches must be extended to examine the shifting public, private and political spaces associated with the current phase of global restructuring.

Much of the feminist critique of globalization discourse is an extension of more general feminist critiques of neo-classical economic theory. Feminists have long argued that the central player in this discourse, the 'sovereign individual', was from its conception a male. Early liberal and capitalist discourse constituted men as sovereign individuals and women as the dependants of fathers and husbands (Abbott and Wallace, 1992: 5). Others have argued that the neo-classical vision misrepresents economic relations and processes because it fails to account for the gendered division of labour and the production and reproduction of human resources (see especially Elson, 1991 and 1992). Waring's work, in particular, demonstrates how the phallocentrism informing neo-classical economics, and the patriarchal assumptions embedded in its construction of the economy, disadvantage women by failing to account for their unpaid labour in the home and community (Waring, 1988).

Feminist conceptual analyses of the discourse of restructuring have tended to follow a similar trajectory. It is argued that this discourse conceals women's experience of restructuring precisely because it assumes that women's unpaid labour is infinitely elastic, and thus capable of covering for shifts and shortfalls of resources previously acquired elsewhere (Elson, 1987). Others have questioned globalization discourse on the grounds that it continues to assume that women's paid labour supplements that of the male breadwinner; that women's reproductive labour is unproductive labour; and that the informal sector does not contribute to the economy (Williams, 1992: 12–14). These and other critiques have led feminist economists to argue for a 'gender-sensitive' analysis which would better demonstrate the differential impacts of structural adjustment on women and men.

Most of the empirical research on the gendered dimensions of restructuring has been conducted in developing countries, where the effects of structural adjustment policies have been most obvious and severe. One recent study conducted for the US Agency for International Development (USAID), for example, indicates that stabilization and adjustment policies have had five primary negative consequences for women. First, evidence everywhere demonstrates that poverty is increasingly gendered. The so-called 'feminization of poverty' is particularly acute among female-headed households and elderly women. Second, women have acted as 'shock-absorbers' during adjustment by curtailing their own consumption and increasing their workload to compensate for household income loss. Third, women tend to be more directly affected by reductions in social welfare spending and public programmes. Privatization and welfare cuts often simply mean that social services are shifted from the paid to the unpaid labour of women. Fourth, gains made toward the goal of gender equality during the 1970s are being eroded due to shifts in the employment market and reductions in child care, education and retraining programmes. Finally, public expenditure constraints have a direct impact on women's employment and working conditions due to the relatively high representation of women in public-sector occupations (Mayatech Corporation, 1992: xiv).

If, as Soja argues, restructuring evokes 'sequential combinations of falling apart and building up again', then clearly gender is integral to this process. In developing countries, structural adjustment has signalled a shift from the exploitation of primary resources to labour-intensive manufacturing, especially through the creation of export-processing zones (EPZs). These zones, characterized by selective incentives for industry and weak regulatory regimes for workers, enable the governments of newly industrializing countries (NICs) to compete for foreign investment in export-oriented manufacturing. Indeed, according to the discourse of restructuring, it is precisely the competition provided by NICs that has forced the restructuring of core manufacturing sectors and the rationalization of its labour force.

However, the gendered foundations of these shifts remain unacknowledged and invisible, even though it is women workers who are disproportionately represented in the export-led manufacturing sector. These women work at near or below subsistence wages and without the benefits of training or the protection of labour and safety regulations (Spivak, 1989: 223). They produce consumer goods but rarely consume them and, to the extent that the nation-state mediates their experience, it is to facilitate their exploitation directly by multinational corporations and indirectly by affluent Western, often women, consumers. This division of labour, in turn, has had a profound impact on gender relations, the production and reproduction of human resources, and the stability of family and community life. Within core countries, trade unions and policy-makers have focused on restructuring in the manufacturing sector and the associated decline in high-wage skilled jobs and full-time employment. The burden of deindustrialization in these countries has fallen on men, who disproportionately filled the ranks of the unionized manufacturing sector (Cohen, 1992: 109–10). The long-term, if not permanently, high levels of unemployment among this workforce has eroded previous assumptions about the primary role of the male breadwinner, cyclical unemployment and social insurance schemes.

Policy-makers' seemingly singular concern with structural adjustment in the manufacturing sector (the falling apart), however, ignores the gendered dimensions of the building up again. It is women who have moved into the growing sales and service sectors and it is women who have adjusted to the decline of full-time employment. Women have also adjusted to the efficiencies provided by minimum-wage jobs, the explosion of part-time employment, and the re-emergence of home-work. Family incomes are dropping while both the number of paid hours to support a household and the number of female-headed single-parent families have increased dramatically. All of these factors combine to entrench and accelerate the ghettoization of women workers in low-wage sectors, and the feminization of poverty.

Although these have been the general tendencies, women's experience of structural adjustment in core economies is also fractured and polarized around race and class. For example, immigrant women and women with less education have been adversely affected by deindustrialization in the clothing and garment industries, and cuts to job-retraining programmes discourage their successful re-entry into the labour force. At the same time, however, there has been an increase of women in managerial and other professional occupations. These women, to lessening degrees, have been sheltered from the gendered impacts of restructuring and are often able to manage increased workforce participation and family responsibilities by employing women who have been displaced and marginalized by the adjustment process. Within core economies, the burden of adjustment has largely been carried by working-class, less educated, and immigrant women.

'Gender-sensitive' empirical research, then, has demonstrated the unequal, contradictory and gendered underpinnings of restructuring on a national and global scale. Too often, however, these analyses operate under the assumption that replacing 'bad' phallocentric discourse and gender-blind research with 'good' gender-sensitive theory and evidence will prompt states to develop policies designed to reverse the negative impacts of restructuring on women. This assumption, I think, conveys questionable impressions. The first is that unequal gender impacts are accidental rather than integral to the current round of restructuring. The second is that the state is outside the restructuring process and, therefore, able to neutralize its gendered effects.

In the next section of this chapter, I shall argue that this kind of gender-sensitive research fails to theorize sufficiently the process of restructuring and the role of the state in constituting and reconstituting gender relations to conform to the new 'social mould'. The current round of restructuring represents a fundamental shift in regimes of accumulation and with it a change in institutional practices, regulatory regimes, norms and behaviours – in other words, the simultaneous realignment of the economic, social and political. A feminist analysis must begin with the premise that restructuring represents a struggle over the appropriate boundaries of the public and private, the constitution of gendered subjects within these spheres and, ultimately, the objects of feminist political struggle. In order to better understand the current round of boundary shifting, however, it is instructive to recount how previous liberal-capitalist regimes' constructions of the public and the private helped define both women as political subjects and the limits of politics.

Shifting the boundaries

Capitalism and its ideological ally liberalism have always been constructed and reconstructed through the 'art of separation', which drew politically negotiated boundaries through the social mould. The very development of these systems depended on fracturing the feudal social mould into a series of tangible and symbolic spaces, each governed by its own rules and procedures. The Church was divided from the state so that it could be governed by the principles of liberalism. The state was separated from the economy so that the market could develop according to the requisites of capitalism, free from political interference. Finally, a line was drawn between the public and the private so that the family remained the responsibility of the male breadwinner – the individual patriarch (Waltzer, 1984: 315–30).

Classical liberalism prescribed and then realized a reorganization of metaphorical, economic, social and political space. In so doing, it reorganized the framework through which social power was expressed (Harvey, 1989: 255). It put sovereignty in the hands of a new social agent – the citizen – who exercised limited power through the institutions of liberal democracy. At the same time, however, classical liberalism profoundly contracted political space and the legitimate objects of politics. Its combined doctrines of *laissez faire* and the negative state 'constructed the market as immune from state interference' (MacKinnon, 1989: 190). Similarly, the public–private split protected the rule of the individual patriarch from the gaze of the state. The realm of the private – of personal and family life – was, in custom and law, sacred ground upon which the state could not tread. It was simply assumed that women were subject to the rule of men: a 'man's home was his castle' (Pateman, 1985: 192).

Classical liberalism, as feminist theorists have long argued, was and continues to be a phallocentric and contradictory discourse. Although it constructed the citizen in universal terms, it was in its conception a 'gender-political' concept (Fraser, 1989: 123). The public–private divide effectively meant that only men could become citizens and claim the rights of freedom and equality in the public sphere, while women were deemed the natural subjects of men in the private sphere (Siim, 1988: 162). The system constructed women as 'pre-political' subjects, while the rigid boundary between the public and private served to 'privatize' and individualize women's oppression. Women's condition was not part of the legitimate political agenda. Women's political agency for most of the reign of classical liberalism, then, was directed toward gaining recognition as liberal-democratic citizens and making the politics of their 'private' lives part of the public terrain. It was, in effect, a political battle fought at the boundaries of classical liberalism's public and private divide.

Although there is widespread consensus among feminist scholars about the manner in which classical liberalism constituted gendered political subjects and constrained the objects of political struggle, there is less agreement about the effects of the welfare state on women. The welfare state emerged as a particular response to tendencies of *laissez faire* capitalism to crisis. It was an instance of restructuring which fundamentally realigned the boundaries between the economy and the state as well as the public and private systems (Fraser, 1989: 129). The welfare state was the culmination of a protracted crisis and political struggle conducted by, among others, women and workers. It realized a radical expansion of the public by claiming responsibility for activities that were previously deemed as private either in the sense of the private sector or the family (Andrew, 1984: 667). The Keynesian welfare state intervened in the economy through regulation and direct participation, and at the same time politicized private relations, opening the family and other aspects of private life to new forms of state scrutiny and assistance (Gotell, 1990). In so doing, it created new spaces for politics and new constructions of citizenship.

It is widely recognized that the welfare state fundamentally changed the condition of women as mothers, workers and citizens. The social safety net, support services and increased opportunities for employment in the state system made women's lives more secure, and decreased or eliminated their economic dependency on individual men (Piven, 1990: 254). At the same time, however, it has been argued that this state form was equally gendered and patriarchal. The welfare state introduced the concept of social citizenship, but the social safety net was constructed as a gendered and hierarchical system. Men were interpolated into the system largely through contributory schemes which enabled them to claim their 'right' to social insurance. Women, by and large, were interpolated into a different category and social role – that of the welfare client and dependency on the state (Fraser, 1989: 129, 147). Moreover, the role of 'welfare client' was deeply inscribed with patriarchal assumptions including, among others, the family wage, women's dependence on men, the gendered division of labour, women's primary role as carers, and women's access to self-determination. There is a strong body of feminist thought, therefore, which interprets the development of the welfare state as merely a transition from 'private' to 'public' or state patriarchy (Brown, 1981). This view emphasizes that women were the objects of the welfare state and the victims of patriarchy, regardless of state form.

There is an equally persuasive body of literature, however, which provides a more complex interpretation of women's relationship with the welfare state. For these theorists, the welfare state was a form of public patriarchy as well as a source of women's empowerment. In particular, Siim argues that women were empowered as a group to the extent that the welfare state recognized its responsibilities for social reproduction and constructed a 'social citizenship', that is, universal rights of the citizen vis-à-vis the state. The politicization of the private provided women with new resources, whether through the direct participation of women as public employees, the proliferation of public agencies regulating social reproduction, or a conception of citizenship which allowed women to make collective demands on the state (Siim, 1988: 174, 179). In other words, it was precisely women's dependency on the welfare state that enabled them to organize to make collective claims and to identify the state as the object of their political struggle. The welfare state, as Fraser puts it, brought new forms of social control, but in so doing created new forms of conflict, new social movements and new conflict zones (Fraser, 1989: 132).

According to this perspective, then, women were active participants in the politicization of the private, which, in turn, gave them a new public space to struggle collectively for an expanded welfare state. This space enabled women to negotiate welfare policy to make it more responsive to women's needs and, more generally, to demand state action to improve the condition of women within the state, the family and the workplace. These projects, in turn, gave rise to a myriad of organizations which mobilized women to make collective demands on the state, established new political coalitions and lines of conflict, and inserted the women's movement into political struggles which were not immediately tied to the social welfare system. For example, the women's movement at present is a key component of the broad-based international coalition opposing the social consequences of globalization (Cox, 1991: 335).

Recent analyses, then, suggest that the contemporary women's movement, like the suffrage movement before it, had an interactive and productive relationship with the mode of regulation – state form – and the historically contingent negotiation of the boundary between the public and the private. The examples of the *laissez faire* liberal and welfare states indicate that restructuring entails a struggle over the constitution of the public–private divide. In turn, the outcome of this struggle has been critical for women in terms of how they are interpolated into politics, the political spaces open to them, and the objects of their political struggle.

It is clear that the current moment of restructuring can be viewed as a concerted discursive and political struggle around the very meaning of the public and private. The proponents of globalization seek radically to shrink the public – the realm of political negotiation – and, at the same time, expand and reassert the autonomy of the private sector and the private sphere. This neo-conservative or 'hyper-liberal' political vision seeks to dismantle the Keynesian welfare state and return to nineteenth-century *laissez faire* liberalism (Cox, 1991: 342). It promises to reduce the state to a 'rigid political shell', and empower flexible and competitive market forces to generate a new social order (Drache and Gertler, 1991: 7).

Michel Foucault has argued that 'the state consists in the codification of a whole number of power relations' and that a 'revolution is a different type of codification of the same relations' (Held et al., 1983: 312–13). From this perspective, the politics of restructuring represents a revolution – one that is still in progress but, nonetheless, seeks to recode the realm of the political constituted by the Keynesian welfare state. At this point, it is unclear whether this revolution will be either total or successful. Even more problematic is how it will affect the constitution of women as political subjects or the objects of their political struggles. Nevertheless, we are engaged in a process of recodification: the logic and limits of the politics of the welfare state have passed.

The contraction of the political realm of the welfare state has occurred on a number of interrelated levels. First and foremost, international trading agreements and the globalization of capital both pre-empt and reduce the capacities of national governments to enforce democratically negotiated responses to pressures on national economies. Paradoxically (or not), this is an era which extols the democratic citizen and, at the same time, reduces the terrain of his sovereignty. Second, the erosion of the sovereignty of nation-states has been accompanied by discursive representations which assign primacy to the market and render political mediation impossible. This discourse posits the process of restructuring as an inescapable necessity which demands that previous definitions of the common good, such as social welfare, be replaced with market liberal definitions such as 'efficiency' and 'competition'. The effect is to depoliticize the economic by representing it as self-regulating and directive. Third, and more tangibly, the reduction of the state through deregulation, privatization and programme cuts restricts and reassigns the spaces for politics and political agency. All of these factors attempt to 'reprivatize' what was once public and, in doing so, create new norms and expectations about what is 'up for grabs' in politics and, ultimately, about the role of the citizen.

Although these shifts have invariably been supported and accomplished without reference to gender, this realignment of the public and the private obviously has profound implications for women and the women's movement as constituted by the welfare state. From the beginning, the neo-conservative agenda of reducing the state and unfettering the market has been recognized as conflicting with the equity agenda of the women's movement. The contemporary women's movement has envisioned an increased role for the state both through an elaboration of the social welfare net and the regulation of the private sector. Universal and affordable child day care, income security for single mothers and elderly women, and affirmative action in the workplace, for example, all demand more government intervention and not less as the neo-conservatives have promised (Gotell and Brodie, 1991: 62). These incompatible visions about the role of the state have informed the gender gap in most Western party systems since the emergence of neo-conservatism.

The political ascendancy of neo-conservatism has placed many women's organizations in the paradoxical position of defending the same social welfare system that they had previously criticized for its patriarchalism, classism, and racism and as an agency of social control (Abbott and Wallace, 1992: 22). Nevertheless, with the progressive dismantling of the welfare state, this political strategy becomes less paradoxical than self-defeating. The boundary shifting associated with this round of restructuring has eroded the political spaces from which the contemporary women's movement found much of its cohesion and empowerment. Social welfarism in its familiar patriarchal form is being rapidly taken off the political agenda. At the same time, the so-called private realm is being reconstituted. This reconstruction is premised on what Fraser calls a reprivatization discourse which seeks to repatriate the economic and the social to their former domestic and official economic enclaves (Fraser, 1989: 172). Reprivatization of the domestic, in particular, has been accompanied by efforts to revitalize and reconstruct the hetero-patriarchal family. This discourse can be discerned most obviously in neo-conservative rhetoric which blames both the welfare state and feminism for the breakdown in the social and moral fabric. It views the family as the fundamental building block in the new order, asserting that families should look after their own, and that state policies should act to make sure that they do (Abbott and Wallace, 1992: 2). Regardless of rhetoric, reprivatization is being enforced through privatization and welfare cuts which effectively off-load social repro-duction to the private sphere.

Gender-sensitive research suggests that reprivatization rests on the patriarchal assumption that these responsibilities can be transferred from the paid to unpaid work of women; but I believe that there is more at work here. Reprivatization discourse is increasingly framed in terms of a new definition of citizenship which denies that the citizen can claim universal social rights from the state. The new common good is one which promotes efficiency and competition. In turn, the good citizen is one who recognizes the limits and liabilities of state intervention and, instead, works longer and harder in order to become self-reliant (Drache, 1992: 221). According to this vision, those who make group claims for compensatory justice, such as the women's movement, are isolated as 'special interest groups', who demand privileges that are unearned, and violate the new norms of citizenship.

Birte Siim argues that the state has nowhere been neutral to women, and that the blurred outline of the reconstituting liberal-democratic state appears to be no exception (Siim, 1988: 160). But, also like its predeces-sors, it is fraught with contradictions and instabilities which open new political spaces and opportunities for what Foucault calls 'subversive recodifications' (Held et al., 1984: 313). In many ways, the patriarchal assumptions that inform the move to reprivatization also construct a vision of the private which is no longer sustainable. The nuclear family is no longer the dominant family form. Indeed, in some countries, the female-headed single-parent family is as common as the 'idealized' male breadwinner model (Fraser, 1989: 149). Moreover, the notion of a single family wage has virtually disappeared as more and more women, single and married, are forced into the labour market in order to sustain family life. Put differently, the women are not at home, and the changing economic order promises to keep it that way.

Although reprivatization discourse envisions the reconstruction of the private according to the model of nineteenth-century liberalism, the economic and structural foundations for this recoding have disappeared just as surely as the horse and buggy. But the women's movement must also realize that the foundations for the Keynesian welfare state, replete with its patriarchal assumptions about the gendered division of labour, also have crumbled. This being said, the new order has not devised a coherent plan for social reproduction. Indeed, its phallocentric and patriarchal underpinnings appear to blind it to a fundamental contradiction. It places women simultaneously in the workforce and in the home. This provides a formula for a crisis in social reproduction.

Restructuring is a moment of maximal change which evokes ruptures in systems of representation, cultural forms, and governing philosophies (Harvey, 1989: 238). This rupture has eroded the Fordist model of social reproduction, closing familiar spaces for the women's movement, but in turn opening others. While it is always risky to look into the future, this may be the moment when the women's movement can assert a model of social citizenship and social reproduction that is free from its previous patriarchal underpinnings. The coming crisis in social reproduction may indeed provide the discursive space to recode the terrain of the private from women's dependency to, as Fraser puts it, a politics of social needs (Fraser, 1989: ch. 8).

To sum up, I have argued in this chapter that the current round of restructuring involves a fundamental realignment of the social, economic and political. This process is far from complete: neither is it inevitable as neo-conservative discourse suggests. What is clear, however, is that the passing of the welfare state, the erosion of the public and the simultaneous valorization of the private, disrupt and displace both the sites and objects of political struggle for women and all disadvantaged groups. The phallocentric underpinnings of neo-classical economics and neo-conservative politics act to conceal the impacts of restructuring on the everyday lives of women and men. Yet, neither displacement of the economies of adjustment on gendered subjects nor the closing of familiar political spaces is likely to forestall the contradictions of this emerging social order, especially as they relate to reproduction of human resources. The political terrain and strategic goals of the women's movement have shifted, but they have not disappeared.

References

Abbott, Pamela and Claire Wallace (1992) *The Family and the New Right*. Pluto Press, Boulder, Co.

Andrew, Caroline (1984) 'Women and the Welfare State'. In *Canadian Journal of Political Science*, December.

Brodie, Janine (forthcoming) 'The Constitutional Confidence Game: The Economic Union Proposals and the Politics of Restructuring'.

Brown, Carol (1981) 'Mother's, Father's and Children: From Private to Public Patriarchy'. In Lydia Sargent (ed.) *Women and Revolution*. Black Rose Press, Montreal.

Clarkson, Stephen (1991) 'Disjunctions: Free Trade and the Paradox of Canadian Development'. In Daniel Drache and Meric Gertler (eds), *The New Era of Global Competition: State Policy and Market Power*. McGill-Queen's University Press, Montreal.

Cohen, Marcy (1992) 'The Feminization of the Labour Market: Prospects for the 1990s'. In Daniel Drache (ed.) *Getting on Track: Social Democratic Strategies for Ontario*. McGill-Queen's Press, Kingston, Ont.

Cox, Robert (1991) 'The Global Political Economy and Social Choice'. In Daniel Drache and Meric Gertler (eds), *The New Era of Global Competition: State Policy and Market Power*. McGill-Queen's University Press, Montreal.

Drache, Daniel (ed.) (1992) 'Conclusion'. In Daniel Drache (ed.) *Getting on Track: Social Democratic Strategies for Ontario*. McGill-Queen's University Press.

Drache, Daniel and Meric Gertler (1991) 'The World Economy and the Nation-State: The New International Order'. In Daniel Drache and Meric Gertler (eds) *The New Era of Global Competition*. McGill–Queen's University Press, Montreal.

Elson, Diane (1987) 'The Impact of Structural Adjustment on Women'. Commonwealth Secretariat, London.

——— (1991) *Male Bias in the Development Process*. Manchester University Press, Manchester.

——— (1992) 'From Survival Strategies to Transformation Strategies'. In Lourdes Beneria and Shelley Feldman (eds) *Unequal Burden: Economic Crises, Personal Poverty and Women's Work*. Westview Press, Boulder, Co.

Fraser, Nancy (1989) *Unruly Practices: Power, Discourse and Gender in Contemporary Social Theory*. University of Minnesota Press, Minneapolis.

Friedman, Harriet (1991) 'New Wines, New Bottles: The Regulation of Capital on a World Scale'. In *Studies in Political Economy*, no. 36, Autumn.

Gotell, Lise (1990) 'Women, Party Politics and Neo-Conservatism in Canada'. Paper presented at the 1990 Annual Meeting of the Canadian Political Science Association, Victoria, British Columbia.

Gotell, Lise and Janine Brodie (1991) 'Women and Parties: More Than an Issue of Numbers'. In Hugh Thorburn (ed.) *Party Politics in Canada*. Prentice-Hall, Toronto.

Grosz, Elizabeth (1990) 'Philosophy'. In Sneja Gunew (ed.) *Feminist Knowledge: Critique and Construct*. Routledge, New York.

Harder, Sandra (1992) *Economic Restructuring in Canada: Developing a Gender-Sensitive Analytic Framework*. Status of Women in Canada, Ottawa.

Harvey, David (1989) *The Condition of Postmodernity*. Basil Blackwell, Oxford.

Held, David et al. (eds) (1984) *State and Society in Contemporary Britain: A Critical Introduction*. Polity Press, Cambridge.

Lipietz, Alain (1987) *Mirages and Miracles*. Verso, London.

——— (1988) 'Reflections on a Tale'. In *Studies in Political Economy*, 26, Summer.

MacKinnon, Catherine (1989) *Towards a Feminist Theory of the State*. Harvard University Press, Cambridge, Mass.

Mayatech Corporation (1992) 'Gender and Adjustment'. Office of Women and Development, US Agency for International Development, Washington DC.

Pateman, Carole (1985) *The Sexual Contract*. Polity Press, Cambridge.

Piven, Frances Fox (1990) 'Ideology and the State: Women, Power, and the Welfare State'. In Linda Gordon (ed.) *Women, the State, and Welfare*. University of Wisconsin Press, Madison.

Siim, Birte (1988) 'Toward a Feminist Rethinking of the Welfare State'. In Kathleen Jones and Anna Jonasdottir (eds) *The Political Interests of Gender*. Sage Publications, Newbury Park.

Soja, Edward (1989) *Postmodern Geographies*. Verso, London.

Spivak, G.C. (1989) 'The Political Economy of Women as Seen by a Literary Critic'. In Elizabeth Weed (ed.) *Coming to Terms: Feminism, Theory and Politics*. Routledge, New York.

Walzer, Michael (1984) 'Liberalism and the Art of Separation'. In *Political Theory*, August.

Waring, Marilyn (1988) *If Women Counted: A New Feminist Economics*. Harper and Row, San Francisco.

Williams, Marjorie (1992) 'Gender and Economic Policies in the Context of Structural Adjustment and Change: The Productivity Link'. North–South Institute Workshop, Ottawa.

4

Structural Adjustment, Demographic Change and Population Policies: Some Preliminary Notes

Caren Grown

The relationship between structural adjustment and population policy is of great importance to those concerned with sustainable economic growth, development, and the satisfaction of basic needs and livelihoods of healthy populations. As noted by Ingrid Palmer (1991), one of the few to write on this topic, 'if the ultimate goal of adjustment is to raise per capita production, income and living standards, then the policy instruments chosen for the strategy should encourage such resource deployment and contingent fertility decisions as would not dissipate economic gains in the long term.' In other words, the policies that attempt to influence the parameters of population growth and economic growth should be in step with each other. However, as will be seen in the African case (and perhaps in other regions as well), there are grounds for believing that the typical package of economic policy instruments does not encourage this congruence. Deterioration of women's economic status, by leading to further uncertainty, locks women even more tightly into survival strategies which emphasize fertility and dependency. Palmer (1991: 4) explains it well:

> Old sources of insecurity are aggravated; any hope of providing for old age with economic resources recedes further. As family resources become scarcer, discrimination against girls in nutrition, education and health expenditure increases. More limited productive assets for women means greater labor exploitation to maintain living standards. With diminishing chances of surplus economic accumulation and less ability to plan for a better future, women may retreat into their traditional role of motherhood for securing labor assistance and old age support.

This brief note attempts to introduce a set of preliminary hypotheses concerning the relationship between structural adjustment, fertility trends and population policies. These hypotheses are speculative, largely because few good studies exist of the relationship between structural adjustment, population policies and demographic change; the data necessary for this task are either non-existent in many countries or of quite poor quality. Another issue is timing – there is a lag of several years before the full effects of these economic policies on demographic variables can be determined. Researchers in other forums have emphasized the importance of separating out the effects of economic crisis from the effects of policies that respond to those crises (Reher and Ortega Osona, 1992; Guzman Molina, 1992). This is an important consideration in the analysis of population data. Needed for this task are good anthropological studies of fertility decisions, which will help guide hypothesis development. We shall return to these points later.

Demographic behaviour and economic growth

The relationship between demographic behaviour and economic growth has been an object of study since Malthus and Marx. Since that time, studies on these linkages have evolved through numerous phases. Early explanations of the demographic transition in different countries stressed the role of per-capita income growth in reducing, first, mortality and then fertility rates (Easterlin, 1980). Current thinking stresses that, if poverty (expressed in low per-capita income) is the main factor underlying high death and birth rates, the solution is economic growth, aided by strong family programmes. Others argue that rapid population growth has an adverse impact on growth in per-capita income through a variety of mechanisms, such as a reduction in domestic savings rates and diversion of funds away from productive investment (National Academy of Sciences, 1971). In this paradigm, economic growth, when combined with family planning, is both necessary and sufficient for reducing population growth.

The 1970s and 1980s were marked by considerable rethinking about the relationship between population growth and economic development. To date, however, little consensus has been reached on whether that relationship is positive, negative or neutral. Nor is there consensus on the larger issue of causation: does economic growth induce fertility decline or does population growth induce poverty and inhibit economic development?

The demographic transition and structural adjustment

Since the 1960s and 1970s population growth rates have decreased almost everywhere except in sub-Saharan Africa, but in global terms demographic pressures require serious policy reflection. Overall, fertility has decreased from 3.8 births per woman in the period 1975–80 to 3.3 in 1990–95 (UNFPA, 1993). In Latin America and the Caribbean, fertility dropped from 5.5 in the period 1965–70 to 3.6 in 1985–90. The Asian trends are similar, with fertility declining from 6.1 births per woman in the period 1970–75 to 4.6 in 1985–90. Sub-Saharan Africa, after decades of high child-bearing rates, shows only a small drop over the past twenty years, and at 6.2 births per woman, fertility rates remain much higher than in other regions.[1]

Nonetheless, by the end of the 1990s, the world population is expected to be 6.26 billion, up from 5.57 billion in 1993 (UNFPA, 1993). The demographic momentum engendered by past and current growth rates carries larger and larger waves of human increase, in terms of sheer numbers, even as growth rates decline. Between 1990 and 2010, the world's population is expected to increase by one-third. In the context of this volume's focus, it becomes necessary to reflect on the potential relationship between macro-economic policy initiatives, such as Structural Adjustment and liberalization, and the mounting pressures of population growth.

Few authors have attempted to analyse empirically the relationship between adjustment and demographic variables. The International Union for the Scientific Study of Population (IUSSP) held a conference in October 1992 on the demographic consequences of structural adjustment in Latin America. Many of the studies are preliminary and offer only tentative evidence.[2] Several other micro-level studies make passing reference to fertility changes within the context of adjustment.[3] The relationship between adjustment and fertility, however, has not been rigorously analysed. The following section presents some hypotheses derived from these studies, but as yet lacking scientific testing.

Consequences of greater poverty for demographic variables

The consequences of greater Third World poverty for demographic trends are not entirely clear, and the effects are likely to differ by region.[4] One hypothesis is that poverty acts as a strong deterrent to a decline in the fertility rate. For example, poverty is likely to hamper the trend toward fertility decline in a variety of ways: shrinking economies will probably hinder the achievement of gender equality; the persistence of women's subordination may preclude them from being able to implement restrictions in the size of their families; and a large literature now documents the tremendous unmet need for contraception among women of child-bearing age (Bongaarts et al., 1990; Sinding, 1993). With more limited access to resources and in the absence of other channels for self-fulfilment, women may continue to want several children as a source of status, security and gratification.

Some have claimed that cuts in the health sector translate into decreased availability of contraceptive and abortion services (see Cornia et al., 1987). Access to health and education is limited by cuts in government expenditures for social services, and this may inhibit both the motivation and use of means to limit fertility; it is noteworthy that female education is strongly correlated with fertility decline. The imposition of user charges, a key element of structural adjustment, helps to place the burden of reproduction on private citizens. The result is that the poor make less use of services because they cannot afford to pay, with predictable results for infant health and mortality (Palmer, 1991).[5] Even if employment is not cut, salary cuts and wage ceilings lead to more frequent strikes, shorter work days, less money to import contraceptives such as the pill and IUD, and generally affect the quality and quantity of reproductive health services provided (Due, 1991). On the other hand, to the extent that donors finance family-planning programmes, there may be some immunity to the cutbacks (Zeitlin et al., 1994). Shrinking incomes and cuts in social services increase the workload of women inside and outside the home and increase the value of child labour (Elson, 1992). The persistence of high rates of infant and child mortality may lead women to have more children than they may actually want.

Although these factors point to fertility increases, their net effect in Latin America is likely to be a slower or stagnating rate of decline, because the difficulty of providing for children acts as a powerful incentive against child-bearing; other factors, such as increased communications, may stimulate the demand for birth control (Barroso, 1991). But even in Latin America, where the inability to support many children is a strong factor underlying the motivation for birth control, the very conditions associated with poverty can prevent women and men from acting on this motivation.

The demographic possibilities vary according to region, rural/urban status, household structure and so forth. In Africa, Palmer (1991) argues that adjustment policies in agriculture are strongly pro-natalist. This is seen clearly when one includes variables that are part of women's background status or the socio-cultural environment of gender relations. Structural adjustment in agriculture will impose more work on women but grant them less control over a resource and income base for years to come. For urban populations, Palmer claims, adjustment policies will raise the value of children's assistance in the short to medium term. At the same time, more widespread and intense poverty will delay further the chance of investing in the quality of children's lives (for example, in education or nutrition). Also, increasing poverty may result in higher infant and child mortality. Adjustment programmes do not ostensibly help larger proportions of urban populations toward a demographic transition.

There is one other observation that applies across regions. The increasing poverty of the Third World curtails the ability of governments and individuals to finance population programmes. The United Nations medium-term projection for population growth is based on the assumption that by the year 2000, total fertility in the Third World will fall from 3.8 births per woman to 3.3, and the prevalence of contraceptive use will rise from 51 to 59 per cent of couples. To reach this goal, the amount spent on population programmes (broadly conceived) must be doubled from the current level of $4.5 billion annually to $9 billion by the end of the decade.[6] The great difficulty of reaching this target is that more than two-thirds of the $3.5 billion is provided by Third World countries themselves (Barroso, 1991). In an era of constrained public financing, where will governments find these resources?

In sum, declining fertility may be achieved at enormous human cost, both because of the frustration behind the decision not to have a child (due to constrained economic circumstances) and because of the crude methods that are likely to be employed to avoid or interrupt a pregnancy. Simultaneously, fiscal pressures in both donor and recipient countries signal the possibility of fewer resources for population programmes and related infrastructures.

Population policies

Population policies are deliberate efforts by national governments to influence aggregate levels of fertility, mortality and migration (Dixon-Mueller, 1993). They typically include a reproductive policy, a health policy and policies relating to migration and population distribution.

Most population policy statements begin with a rationale of why there is a population problem. For example, current or projected growth rates can hinder the achievement of a country's social and economic objectives, such as hastening economic growth, achieving a better balance of resources, or improving overall living standards by altering demographic behaviour in specified ways. In some cases, timetables and targets are set for their achievement. Finally, policies set out specific measures for implementation, such as improving health and nutrition through community campaigns, slowing rural-to-urban migration by investing in improvements in the agricultural sector, strengthening family planning services, and so on.

The boundaries of a population policy are unclear, for they blend easily and inevitably into more comprehensive social, economic and political policies (Dixon-Mueller, 1993: 16). Although a population policy may set demographic targets, its implementation almost always depends on interlocking sets of social programmes relating to employment, education, health, housing, family welfare, urban planning, and agricultural and industrial growth. Each sectoral programme has its own goals that may complement or contradict the intent of a demographic policy. The policy of granting more family control over agricultural production in China, for example, while achieving the desired result of raising farm output and rural incomes, has encouraged rural couples to have more children despite the official one-child demographic policy (Dixon-Mueller, 1993: 16).

It is common practice for donor agencies, government ministries, or research organizations to develop sophisticated statistical analyses of the characteristics of the development process of a particular country and the impacts of projected population growth rates. These analyses highlight the difficulty of providing universal schooling and health care, raising per-capita incomes, sustaining adequate food production and consumption, and conserving natural resources. The results form the basis of policy proposals. Generally, these models are incomplete as they neglect political constraints confronting decision-makers, such as scarce resources, competing demands, uncertain tenure, and political opposition.

Frequently, the long-term goals of population stabilization and meeting people's basic needs are not linked to structural adjustment goals in a clear and direct way. This is illustrated by population policies in three countries: the Philippines, Brazil and Nigeria. These countries provide interesting examples because all experienced international debt crises resulting in the imposition of economic austerity measures that caused popular unrest. Economic difficulties make implementation of the policies a problem in each of these countries. In Brazil, for example, the Integrated Women's Health Program, designed by feminists, physicians and the government, proved difficult to implement because of the 'deepening economic crisis, spending cuts, and the decentralization of health planning at the state level' (Dixon-Mueller, 1993: 91). The Primary Health Care Program of the Nigerian government is intended to bring health and family-planning services to local populations. User charges levied at all government hospitals under austerity measures, a drop in government expenditures on health care, and inflation have made that goal elusive (Dixon-Mueller, 1993: 96).

Women's agency

So far, this chapter has considered the intersection of structural adjustment and demographic issues without reference to political factors such as the women's movement. In many countries around the world, women activists have resisted both top-down and narrowly conceived demographic policies and structural adjustment programmes (Sen and Grown, 1987). Recent advocacy efforts place women's health concerns and economic objectives in a holistic framework. In September 1992, women's advocates from Latin America, Asia, Africa, the Caribbean, North America and Europe drafted a consensus statement which includes calls to bring structural adjustment and population concerns into alignment and to add women's voices to the development of both macro-economic and population policy. Women's movements in many countries – Brazil, Nigeria, Mexico and others – have called for population policies to be framed within development policies that redress the unequal distribution of resources and power between women and men (International Women's Health Coalition (IWHC), 1993). These movements recognize that global economic crises, structural adjustment policies, and an emphasis on privatization all jeopardize society's ability and willingness to ensure health and education, generate employment, and protect basic human rights.

Conclusion

In the best cases, the purpose of demographic policy is to promote long-term sustainable development and improve the quality of life for all people. Similarly, the purpose of structural adjustment policy is, ostensibly, to raise per-capita production, income and living standards. To quote Palmer (1991), 'the policy interests that are chosen for the strategy should encourage such resource deployment and contingent fertility decisions as would not dissipate economic gains in the long term.' As argued above, there are grounds for believing that the typical package of structural adjustment policy instruments does not encourage this.

At a minimum, more studies like those of Ingrid Palmer and Jose Guzman Molina need to be undertaken to illustrate the intersection of demographic policy and economic policy, and to test some of the hypotheses laid out in the previous sections. At the same time, policy-makers need to consider macro-economic policies which aim at greater human dignity and the elimination of poverty. In the long run, the implementation of these objectives may also hasten the pace of fertility decline, which is one element for a more sustainable future.

Notes

1. Fertility decline is closely associated with both socio-economic development and family-planning-programme efforts. Fertility declines averaging 3.1 children per woman occurred in countries that ranked high on both indexes, while no significant changes were observed in countries that score low on the two indexes (Bongaarts et al., 1990).

2. Reher and Ortega-Osona (1992: 19), in their review of Latin American data for the period 1960–80 find that the links between short-term fluctuation in living standards and demographic behaviour have proved to be tenuous. In another study, Guzman Molina (1992) takes as his starting point the relationship between crisis, structural adjustment and fertility changes. He asks whether the economic crisis and the resulting adjustment programmes have had some measurable effect on the reproductive behaviour of the Latin American population. While insufficient evidence is available to provide categorical answers, Guzman concludes that fertility seems to have decreased more rapidly in the 1980s – in both rural and urban areas – in Latin America than during previous decades.

3. Beneria (1992), for example, notes: 'Our data suggest that the crisis has had an effect on fertility rates; 46.7 percent of the families in the sample had decided either to stop or postpone having children during the 1982–88 period ... Although it is difficult to sort out the effects of the crisis in this respect from those resulting from longer-term fertility trends, [the] connection with the crisis was pointed out by women in the cycle.'

4. The poverty effects of structural adjustment have been documented by Cardoso and Helwege (1992) in Latin America and contributors to Gladwin (1991) in Africa.

5. Schoepf and Engundu (1991) report in their study of Zaire, where structural adjustment programmes have required that all health care be delivered on a fee-for-service basis, that more women are delivered at home.

6. Zeitlin et al. (1994) point out that surprisingly little scientific analysis has been carried out on the financing of population and reproductive health. They note that while total annual resource requirements for population activities by the year 2000 are estimated to vary from $0.6 billion (for the supply of contraceptive commodities) to $11.5 billion (for comprehensive population programmes in 1988 dollars), the accuracy and usefulness of these cost projections are suspect.

References

Barroso, C. (1991) 'Population Policies: Issues and Challenges for the Nineties'. Paper presented at the Harvard University Center for Population and Development Studies, 25 September.

Beneria, L. (1992) 'The Mexican Debt Crisis: Restructuring the Economy and the Household'. In Beneria and Feldman (eds) *Unequal Burden: Economic Crises, Persistent Poverty and Women's Work*. Westview Press, Boulder, Co.

Beneria, L. and S. Feldman (eds) (1992) *Unequal Burden: Economic Crises, Persistent*

Poverty and Women's Work. Westview Press, Boulder, Co.

Bongaarts, J., W.P. Mauldin and J.E. Phillips (1990) 'The Demographic Impact of Family Planning Programs'. In *Studies in Family Planning*, vol. 21, no. 6, 299–310.

Bravo, J. (1992)'The Demographic Consequences of Structural Adjustment: The Case of Chile'. In IUSSP/CEDEPLAR, *The Demographic Consequences of Structural Adjustment in Latin America*, Volumes I and II. International Union for the Scientific Study of Population, Belgium.

Bruce, J. (1989) 'Homes Divided'. In *World Development*, vol. 17, no. 7, July.

Cardoso, E. and A. Helwege (1992) 'Below the Line: Poverty in Latin America'. In *World Development*, vol. 20, no. 1, January, 19–37.

Cornia, G., R. Jolly and F. Stewart (eds) (1987) *Adjustment with a Human Face*. Oxford University Press, Oxford.

Dixon-Mueller, R. (1993) *Population Policy and Women's Rights: Transforming Reproductive Choice*. Praeger Press, Connecticut.

Due, J. (1991) 'Policies to Overcome the Negative Effects of Structural Adjustment Programs on African Female-Headed Households'. In C. Gladwin (ed.), *Structural Adjustment and African Women Farmers*. University of Florida Press, Florida.

Easterlin, R. (1980) *Population and Economic Change in Developing Countries*. University of Chicago Press, Chicago.

Elabor-Idemudia, P. (1991) 'The Impact of Structural Adjustment Programs on Women and their Households in Bendel and Ogun States, Nigeria'. In C. Gladwin (ed.) *Structural Adjustment and African Women Farmers*. University of Florida Press, Florida.

Elson, D. (1992) 'From Survival Strategies to Transformation Strategies.' In Beneria and Feldman (eds) *Unequal Burden: Economic Crises, Persistent Poverty and Women's Work*. Westview Press, Boulder, Co.

Gladwin, C. (ed.) (1991) *Structural Adjustment and African Women Farmers*. University of Florida Press, Florida.

Guzman Molina, J.M. (1992) 'Crisis, Adjustment and Fertility during Latin America's Lost Decade: Facts and Speculations.' In IUSSP/CEDEPLAR, *The Demographic Consequences of Structural Adjustment in Latin America*, Volumes I and II. International Union for the Scientific Study of Population, Belgium.

International Women's Health Coalition (IWHC) (1993) 'Women's Voices '94: Women's Declaration on Population Policies in Preparation for the 1994 International Conference on Population and Development'. IWHC, New York.

IUSSP/CEDEPLAR (1992) *The Demographic Consequences of Structural Adjustment in Latin America*, Volumes I and II. International Union for the Scientific Study of Population, Belgium.

Johnston, B. (1991) 'Getting Priorities Right: Structural Transformation and Strategic Notions'. In C. Gladwin (ed.) *Structural Adjustment and African Women Farmers*. University of Florida Press, Florida.

Lele, U. (1991) 'Women, Structural Adjustment and Transformation: Some Lessons and Questions from the African Experience'. In C. Gladwin (ed.) *Structural Adjustment and African Women Farmers*. University of Florida Press, Florida.

Musgrove, P. (1992) 'Economic Crisis and Health Policy Responses'. In IUSSP/

CEDEPLAR, *The Demographic Consequences of Structural Adjustment in Latin America*, Volumes I and II. International Union for the Scientific Study of Population, Belgium.

National Academy of Sciences (1971) *Rapid Population Growth: Consequences and Policy Implications*, 2 vols. Johns Hopkins University Press, Baltimore.

Palmer, I. (1991) *Gender and Population in the Adjustment of African Economies: Planning for Change*. Women, Work and Development Series, International Labour Office, Geneva.

—— (1992) 'Gender Equity and Economic Efficiency in Adjustment Programs'. In H. Afshar and C. Dennis, *Women and Adjustment in the Third World*. Macmillan, Basingstoke.

Pebley, A. (1992) 'The Use of Surveys to Measure the Impact of Short Term Economic Change on Demographic Variables in Latin America'. In IUSSP/ CEDEPLAR, *The Demographic Consequences of Structural Adjustment in Latin America*, Volumes I and II. International Union for the Scientific Study of Population, Belgium.

Reher, D. and J.A. Ortega Osona (1992) 'Short Run Economic Fluctuations and Demographic Behaviour: Some Examples from Twentieth Century South America'. In IUSSP/CEDEPLAR, *The Demographic Consequences of Structural Adjustment in Latin America*, Volumes I and II. International Union for the Scientific Study of Population, Belgium.

Safa, H. and P. Antrobus (1992) 'Women and the Economic Crisis in the Caribbean'. In L. Beneria and S. Feldman (eds) *Unequal Burden: Economic Crises, Persistent Poverty and Women's Work*. Westview Press, Boulder, Co.

Schoepf, B. and W. Engundu (1991) 'Women and Structural Adjustment in Zaire'. In C. Gladwin (ed.) *Structural Adjustment and African Women Farmers*. University of Florida Press, Florida.

Sen, G. and Caren Grown (1987) *Development, Crises, and Alternative Visions: Third World Women's Perspectives*, Monthly Review Press, New York.

Sinding, S. (1993) 'Estimating Unmet Need'. Paper presented to WHO Meeting on Reproductive Health, Tepotzlan, Mexico.

UNFPA (1993) *The State of World Population 1993*. United Nations Fund for Population Activities, New York.

Waylen, G. (1992) 'Women, Authoritarianism and Market Liberalization in Chile, 1973–1989'. In H. Afshar and C. Dennis, *Women and Adjustment in the Third World*. Macmillan, Basingstoke.

World Bank (1993) *World Bank Development Report 1993: Investing in Health*. Oxford University Press, Oxford.

Zeitlin, J., R. Govindaraj and L. Chen (1994) 'Investing in Reproductive Health'. In G. Sen, A. Germaine and L. Chen, *Population Policy Reconsidered: Health, Empowerment and Human Rights*. Harvard University Press, Cambridge, Mass.

5

Gender, Productivity and Macro-economic Policies in the Context of Structural Adjustment and Change
Marjorie W. Williams

Weak macro-economic performance in many OECD economies has generated a resurgence of the debate around the issues of growth and economic efficiency. The urgent and dominant question of the day is how to expand output growth, improve national standards of living, and maintain international competitiveness. Consequently, macro-economists are now turning their attention to productivity improvement, albeit from a national perspective. The search for the appropriate explanatory and remedial measures to increase economic efficiency and therefore economic growth has once again placed macro-economic policy centre-stage. The immediate response has been to dress up the familiar tools of fiscal and monetary policies in more restrictive garbs. These are then reinforced by programmes of economic liberalization, international and regional trade agreements such as the North American Free Trade Agreement (NAFTA) and the newly consolidated European Single Market. The dress rehearsal for many of the new policies are the International Monetary Fund's and the World Bank's structural adjustment programmes (SAP), which have guided the restructuring of debtor countries over the last ten years.[1]

Long-run solutions to improve the economic performance of key variables, such as capital formation and productivity, centre on mechanisms to streamline macro-economic policies. Predictably, given the focus of macro-economics discussed in the introductory chapter to this book, much of the discussion so far has been conducted in genderless terms. Hence, very little attention has been paid to the role that the economic subordination of women plays in sustaining the economic growth process. Less attention is paid to the relative impact on women and men of past (and proposed new) directional shifts in macro-economic policies.

In this chapter, I shall argue that it is women's labour which has been the great bulwark, stabilizing productivity growth in the world economy.[2] Women's productivity has been the silent factor behind the structural changes and adjustments in both the North and the South. IMF-type structural adjustment programmes and economic liberalization packages now being assembled implicitly depend on women's economic contribution. The main effect of SAP and global restructuring has been to ensure that women are working more hours and with more capital than before. Further economic liberalization, it is argued, will not inherently improve women's economic and social status; rather, there is a strong potential for it to increase the exploitation and marginalization of women both in developed and in developing countries.

That this situation is yet to be recognized by standard economic analysis is no surprise. The undercounting and undervaluation of women's work is fundamental to the economic subordination of women. As Ivan Illich (1982: 4) so aptly puts it, 'of everything that economics measures, women get less'.[3] Nowhere in the arsenal of leading, lagging or coincident indicators is there one that monitors the increasing numbers of unpaid hours women are forced to contribute to support the economy.[4] These hours go toward making up the shortfall in household income, the absence of adequate day-care facilities, and inadequate health-care support.

Macro-economic policy is essentially a byproduct of macro-economic theory (analytically rooted in micro-economic theory) and the social and political environment. But it is economic theory that frequently guides the initiatives of policy-makers. There is, consequently, a need to assess the impact of macro-economic policy on women's lives. Before we can move to the level of engendering economic policy we must first engender economics itself. In this contribution, I propose a reconsideration of two key concepts: productivity and efficiency.

I begin with an initial survey of the literature on the 'dimensions' of productivity, including the debate regarding both the process and the politics of measuring productivity. I then offer an initial exploration into how feminists would begin to reformulate these concepts. The relationship between gender, productivity and macro-economic performance is examined in the next section. I then focus on the link between productivity and macro-economic policy. The final section lays out the beginnings of an alternative framework towards the economic empowerment of women.

The Dimensions of Productivity

According to Ellen Rosen (1984): 'Productivity expresses a relationship between effort and result.'[5] Much of the discussion about productivity centres on the question of efficiency. Typically the concern is with the efficiency with which output is produced by the resources utilized. Effort is a result of the combination of inputs (capital, labour, and so on). Thus, the two main productivity concepts are labour productivity and total (factor) productivity. Labour productivity,[6] which indicates output per person hour, is the mostly widely used. According to Fabricant (1981), it accounts for the fruitfulness of human labour under varying circumstances: labour quality, amount of equipment, scale of output, methods of production. Labour productivity[7] is one example of a class of productivity measures which related output of a 'producing enterprise, industry or economy to one type of input'.

Total (factor) productivity compares total input (tangible and intangible capital, labour, energy, and so on) with total output (see Mark, 1981). Each input is appropriately weighted to account adequately for output per unit of labour and capital. Total productivity that relates output to a combination of inputs shows how efficiently resources as a whole are employed in production. It belongs to a second class of productivity indicators: multifactor measures.

The derivation of productivity series, as with most economic variables, proceeds on the assumption that productivity is technically neutral and genderless. But as Rosen argues: 'Productivity measurement also has a political side ... insofar as it generates "authoritative" statistics, which endow power and can be used to the advantage and disadvantage of interested actors' (1984: 40). As with most statistics, there are controversies over issues of specification and measurement, but the debate remains at the level of specifying the correct functional form. The missing link is gender. Hence, the focus of this chapter is a gender-based re-examination of the theoretical and methodological issues of the productivity debate. Emphasizing gender-based criticism of current productivity analysis must start by deconstructing the definition of productivity and the component variables used in establishing such indices. Since productivity series are determined indirectly by first measuring output and input and then calculating the ratio, an initial starting point is to take a closer look at both the output side and the input side.

Input

On the input side, labour is singled out. Labour input is calculated as the product of the total hours worked and as an index of labour quality. The quality of labour is typically measured by its price or earnings, which in conventional analysis (marginal productivity theory) tends to be equal to its value in production. Thus it would be fair to say that when one kind of labour is more productive than another kind, it will be more valuable and hence will earn more. Emanating from this initial framework are a number of myths and misconceptions that work to the disadvantage of women and the evaluation of their productive contribution to the economy.

In textbooks, students are taught that national resources comprise land, labour, capital and management. Capital is posited as the 'true cost of the economy', eschewing land which in earlier physiocratic economic thought was the source of value, based solely on the criterion that it was seen as the producer of human sustenance. In the classical analysis of Adam Smith and David Ricardo, labour was treated as *the* source of value, the factor capable of producing wealth. Regardless of which factor was pre-eminent at a particular point in time, one truth held: the productivity of the factor was crucial to the well-being of the economy. It was further argued that each factor laid a claim to national production based on its (marginal) productivity. The law of supply and demand and the work–leisure trade-off combined to ensure the highest return to each factor.[8]

Marginal productivity theory further argues that the average compensation per hour provides a good approximation of the workers' marginal product. Wage difference, then, is an accurate reflection of the quality of labour input. Thus the truism develops: higher relative earnings reflect higher relative productivity; more experience reflects higher productivity (human capital theory). What is generally ignored is: (i) discrimination in the labour market that shunts women, as a group, into areas that are then systematically underpaid; and (ii) earnings are affected by institutional arrangement and seniority. Research by Medoff and Abrah (1981) suggests that a 'substantial fraction of the return to experience is unrelated to productivity'. Blau and Kahn, in a recent international study on the gender earnings gap, found that institutional setting in terms of the wage-determining process (centralized or decentralized) and changes in wage structure were of considerable importance over time (Blau and Kahn, 1992).

Another myth is that higher education should be strongly correlated with improved quality of labour and thus with higher relative earnings. Yet, in the case of women, the results do not necessarily tally: it is very often the case that men who have dropped out of high school can end up with more lifetime earnings than college-educated women. Masked behind the myth of lower productivity in the service sector, and the argument that it is harder to improve the productivity of, say, a nurse than an assembly line worker, is the justification of the lower pay of the nurse. Somehow the same logic seems not to apply to the relative earnings of doctors and paraprofessionals in male-dominated areas of the service sector.

Finally, there is the myth that the 'appearance of women decreases the average quality of labour'. This myth is discussed in a number of studies, including Oswald, 1981 (104–6) and Rosow, 1981 (245). Both authors agree that there is a great deal of confusion regarding the emergence of women in the labour market and the downturn in productivity in the US. Of course, a possible explanation might be the confusion of relative earnings with productivity – because women are concentrated in low-paying jobs, this indicates low productivity. The available evidence does not demonstrate this. Ullman (1980) has shown that the image of constantly improving productivity levels in US manufacturing was not due to innovation in products and process, but rather to economies of scale. Thurow (1980: 58) has shown that the industries with the sharpest drop in productivity growth are not those that have a high concentration of women workers.

We are thus faced with the contradictory general proposition that young women workers (in OECD countries) are a source of reduced labour quality and hence a drag on productivity; yet at the same time, their cohorts in the runaway shops of the multinationals of Mexico's *maquiladoras* and the Southeast Asian export-processing zones are sought out for production of components and final products in manufacturing. So we are led to believe that young, inexperienced women workers in the South are vital to global manufacturing but are a drag in other sectors of the economy. Or is the growth of the newly industrialized countries (NICs) based on an anomaly? Are we to assume that women workers in OECD countries work with less capital (both tangible and intangible) than their counterparts in the developing countries?

Output

Productivity measurement generally is presented as if it captures the total effort that goes toward output for a country as a whole (real gross national product). Even sectoral measures do not adequately capture the full contribution of individual sectors towards gross output. Furthermore, some areas of the economy are generally not adequately represented in published productivity series: the governmental sector, construction, services and the household sector.

The problem of market valuation of services provided by governmental bureaucracy[9] and the household sector leads to underrepresentation in aggregate production statistics. Women in both the developed and developing countries are overrepresented in these sectors. Likewise, undervaluation of the service-sector[10] activities dominated by women workers (nursing and auxiliary, clerical and secretarial work in the banking and financial sector) lead to a downward bias in national productivity statistics. Extensive research has been conducted by economists on the complex problem of measuring (both tangible and intangible) capital. The focus is to account for capital's actual contribution to economic output. Far less effort is spent on establishing the contribution of labour and, in particular, women's labour.

Macarov (1982) points to another aspect of the productivity debate that is crucial to women. He argues that increases in productivity are not solely reflected in more output, but that much of the gain from productivity improvement has gone into more leisure time. Not only are women producing more, but many women are working under deteriorating physical and environmental conditions. This is quite evident in developing countries undergoing structural adjustment, where basic services have been drastically reduced. Cash-starved governments encourage the exploitation of women in multinationals' factories. Women in the informal sectors of these countries are also located in areas with the least return, but which require the most gruelling effort. In the OECD countries, women's formal-sector employment has decreased leisure time and extended the working day. Hence, in general, improvement in women's productivity does not always translate into greater monetary rewards or more leisure time but may instead bring more work.

Efficiency

Radical economists have distinguished qualitative and quantitative aspects of efficiency. This distinction has important implications for analysing women's contribution to the economy. Orthodox economists tend to focus on quantitative efficiency, which accordingly represents the greatest possible useful physical output from a given set of physical inputs. Radicals rightly criticize this approach as ahistorical. Gordon (1976) and Mitchell and Watts (1985) focus on qualitative efficiency defined in terms of the ability of the ruling class to reproduce its domination of the social process of production and minimize producers' resistance to ruling-class dominance of the production process. Mitchell and Watts carried this a step forward by suggesting a reformulation on the grounds that the above dichotomy is meaningless if you accept the distinction between labour (actual performance) and labour power (productive capacity). In this context, qualitative efficiency takes on more significance. It now expresses what Mitchell identifies as the maximal extraction of surplus value subjected to alienated labour. Thus qualitative efficiency is located in the sphere of production while quantitative efficiency is located in exchange. This distinction is important because, as Mitchell points out, relying solely on quantitative expressions of efficiency both obscures and mystifies the relations of production (Mitchell and Watts, 1985).

I would argue further that quantitative efficiency obscures and mystifies the crucial linkages between household production and formal sector production, by obscuring the link between production and re-production. Thus the formal economy is able to achieve the ultimate exploitation: extracting increased labour for the same value of labour power (from women) while at the same time making it unmeasurable and thus irrelevant in macro-economic accounting.

Towards a Re-conceptualization of Productivity

As can be seen from the discussion above, productivity analysis has been shrouded in positivism and claims of technical neutrality. Most economists would like to persist in the argument that productivity is a technical matter of assessing effectiveness and hence is politically neu-tral. But like the concept of 'markets' (see Bakker and Elson, Chapters 1 and 2 in this volume) 'production', 'productive' and 'productivity' are also social constructs that need to be critically appraised. To argue, as do marginal-productivity and human-capital theorists, that productivity is primarily determined by demand and supply, disregards too much. It ignores the fact that productivity is socially and culturally determined. We must accept that the behaviour of economic agents can affect the valuation of factor input. When bosses discriminate in hiring practice, pitting one gender against the other, or one race or ethnic group against the other, this can significantly affect the impact of other variables such as education, experience and skill.

Historically, the evaluation of productivity has an inherent male bias. This has contributed to the under-valuation and devaluation of wom-en's work. Yet the reality of economic and social life is that it is women's productivity[11] that has historically cushioned the economy in its long march towards structural adjustment and transformation. Women's labour has been utilized more than ever before in this time of economic crisis. Yet women are paid differently (at a lower income than men) for work of comparable value. Women experience loss of leisure time and therefore a declining standard of living with no extra income for the extra effort that is being extracted from them; there is no fair compen-sation for parting with leisure. What is more pronounced is that women's labour is the only resource whose price does not significantly increase as the demand for its services increases. That is, as the demand for women's productive capabilities increases, there is no commensurate increase in the value of the marginal product.

This is only possible because of the way productivity has been con-ceptualized. It makes women's work invisible and somehow unmeasurable.

At the heart of the controversy regarding the constancy of the wage gap between men and women, and the persistent and pernicious segregation of the labour market, is this issue of productivity. The austere and abstract definition of productivity fails to account adequately for women's work. A new definition, one that is more supportive of women's participation in the economy needs to be fashioned. This is bound to involve conceptual, methodological and technical issues.

The basic step towards productivity decomposition is to recognize the inadequacy of the present two-way grouping used in the aggregation of production: (i) labour–capital; or (ii) skilled–unskilled labour; or (iii) blue collar–white collar, various age categories, among others.[12] These groupings assume that marginal-product theory holds, that economic agents have perfect knowledge and always behave rationally, thereby discounting gender discrimination.

An initial starting point is to focus on the labour–capital grouping. In the literature, a substantial body of research aims at getting the most precise and accurate measure of capital, including the problem of intangible capital; this problem has still not been satisfactorily resolved. Yet, in the case of labour, apart from the distinction between unskilled and skilled, blue- and white-collar, and so on, there are certain obvious deficiencies in the treatment of the labour input. Attempts to sub-aggregate labour and to make the sex composition more adequately reflected in the share of total output and employment are still at a nascent stage. Indeed, much of the research seems to be dedicated to demonstrating that sex composition has a downward bias on productivity because of women's presumed inexperience and/or age. There has been very little focused research on the sex composition of the labour input that does not beg the question. Most studies simply assume that wages reflect productivity weights. This abstracts from the issues of gender discrimination in the labour market.

Women, Macro-economic Performance and Productivity

Currently, there is a large body of literature linking 'good' macro-performance with 'good' productivity.[13] Put simply, 'change in the gross national product is an expression of productivity' (Macarov, 1982: 53). It is therefore not surprising that productivity has become a central concept in the debate surrounding the macro-economic performance of both rich and poor countries. The debate is more open in the OECD countries, especially in the US, where it has become a national preoccupation. But it is no less significant in the countries of the South where the discussion is often masked by issues of structural adjustment for greater productivity.

Lack-lustre productivity is a relevant causal factor in inflation, output and, of course, the level of employment. It is also central to any discussion of international competitiveness. Declining productivity affects international competitiveness via its impact on the price advantage of national goods versus foreign goods. When foreign prices are more favourable than those of national goods the end result is a rising trade deficit and/or decreased economic growth. Increased productivity gains, it is argued, translate into increased standards of living, which affect other social variables such as health care and education, while decreased productivity correlates with inflation.

Since the mid-1960s, there has been a dramatic increase in women's labour-force participation rates worldwide. Global restructuring that shifts production to less developed countries (LDCs) has directly integrated women into manufacturing. Through subcontracting and outsourcing, women's labour is indirectly contributing to the growth and prosperity of OECD manufacturing. In addition, in both the North and the South, structural changes, technological advances and recession have led to an increase in service-sector activity as well as a rise in the economic participation of women. Thus, women's participation in both the formal economy and the household sector doubly contributes to macro-economic performance. Sharon Stichter sums up this argument of the crucial role of women's contribution to national productivity: 'Women's employment seems to be correlated with the rise of industries such as electronics with labor intensive assembly line techniques requiring high levels of managerial control and supervision to achieve high productivity' (Stichter and Parpart, 1990: 19). Other authors have also pointed to the important role played by discipline and control (arising from the technical nature of production) in explaining why electronics manufacturing is so predisposed towards hiring women.

Additionally, I would argue that the casualization of work, women's increased informal-sector activity, and subcontracting or home-based outwork are means of increasing women's productivity and help to bolster macro-economic activity in both the poor and richer countries. Yet this has not been recognized in the current productivity debate. On the contrary, the common trend in the literature is a tendency to identify women's increased participation in the labour force with low national and sectoral productivity. Leichter cites the following: 'the Council of Economic Advisers under the Carter administration estimates that the use of new workers from these groups [women and youths born during the postwar boom] lowered the productivity by a third of a point per year' (Leichter, 1984: 51). The flawed assumption is the myth of women workers' low productivity, supposedly due to age, inexperience, and less skill. Although Leichter does not support the Council of Economic Advisers thesis, it is widely and uncritically quoted in a number of papers and other studies. Obviously, this and other reports implicitly assume the universality of the wage-productivity myth, and abstract from wage discrimination and job-placement discrimination in their analysis. Women are in low-wage jobs not because they have inherent low productivity, or low skill, or no experience, but because of discriminatory market forces.

Thurow (1980) attacks this low productivity of women workers by pointing out that if inexperienced workers were at the heart of the productivity problem, the biggest productivity decline should have occurred in the industries that hire most women and young workers. The industries experiencing sharp reductions in productivity growth are not, however, the industries that hire a lot of women and young people. This myth of women's low productivity could also be refuted by the fact that highly innovative industries (such as electronics) rely on female labour (in off-shore production facilities) for their finished systems and components. I would therefore argue that rather than being a drag on national productivity, women's labour power is a source of dynamic comparative advantage.

In sum, I would agree with Blinder that 'over the long-run the economic performance of any nation depends on its rate of productivity growth and that all factors contribute to economic growth' (Blinder, 1990). But I would go one step further and argue that women's labour contributes doubly, once account is taken of (i) women's labour provided to the formal economy, and (ii) social reproduction – child-rearing and household production (which is both a social and technical process).

Women, Productivity and Macro-economic Policy

If economics neglects a proper count of women's economic contribution to national productivity and total output, then we must expect economic policy to be, at best, indifferent to women or, in the worst case, to have disproportionately negative effects on women. Since policymakers do not start with the presumption of a distinct contribution by women to economic activity, then hardly any allowance is made for the asymmetric effect of macro-economic policy on women.

Macro-economic policy is the set of strategies, principles and rules pursued by a government to achieve low inflation, high-output growth, high employment and an acceptable balance of payments. Successful achievement of these goals hinges on the behaviour of aggregate demand

and aggregate supply. Productivity is crucial to both of these. As Paul Krugman so cogently expressed it: 'productivity isn't everything, but in the longrun it is almost everything' (Passall, 1992: 1). Macro-economic policy at its best seeks to fine-tune the economy to provide the overall stability that will create increased productivity, increased output and, hence, an increased standard of living. Macro-economic policy has been inherently stimulating and has spurred women's productivity in house-hold production, the formal and the informal sectors. Thus women's productivity is a significant contribution to total output and all key macro-economic variables. So even when the particular policy fails to achieve the desired result, women's labour silently makes the difference.

Apart from the reports on women and structural adjustment, a very good example of women's crucial role vis-à-vis economic policy results can be seen in the US. The devastating effect of the Reagan supply-side policy on families was offset by women's labour. As reported by Peter Passell, most of the continuing gains in living standards during the Reagan years came from the fact that more women were putting more hours into paying jobs. The same scenario holds for women living under structural adjustment programmes in poor countries (see Afshar and Dennis, 1992).

The fact that macro-economists are now turning their attention to issues of productivity has significant implications for the direction of, and potential impact on, women's lives. Fiscal and monetary instru-ments are designed to affect economic growth by altering (primarily) aggregate demand and aggregate supply conditions. These include gov-ernment investment decisions, minimum wage policy, tax changes and interest-rate policy. All of these decisions are ultimately informed by economic insights about productivity of labour and capital and the behaviour of aggregated supply and aggregate demand.

Fiscal instruments

The attitude of policy-makers and macro-economists to what is proper fiscal policy reflects their views on the primary factors contributing to growth of output. Typically, the focus is capital (more specifically, growth in the capital stock). If the problem is an inadequate rate of growth, the resulting policy prescription would favour some form of tax relief for capital. For women, the result is not essentially different if the challenge is to spur lagging aggregate demand via a tax cut. In either case, the net effect is a shortfall in government revenue which must somehow be offset. Whether the tax relief was in the form of a tax credit on struc-ture or equipment, or a tax cut on corporate income, the net result may be an implicit increase in the tax burden on the poor.[14] The implicit tax accrues as a result of loss of benefits, and loss of earning as the government reduces expenditure by laying off workers and cutting social services. Hence women will have to work harder by doing more part-time work and increasing household maintenance.

Likewise, emphasis on capital spending on the grounds that a decline in the capital–labour ratio is the main cause of economic slowdown would seem to be a gender-neutral position.[15] But even if the capital–labour ratio has fallen for the economy as a whole, it has been rising for women as a group, both in the household sector and in the labour market. Nonetheless, on the basis of the aforementioned argument, government will be counselled to increase its spending on infrastructure and subsidies to corporations. Since government budgets are finite, there is bound to be a trade-off. More often than not, the programmes to be reduced or eliminated will be those that benefit women.

Monetary instruments

The primary mechanism for stabilizing the macro-economy is manipulation of the money supply and interest rates. Nowhere is gender-neutrality assumed to be stronger than with regard to money; hence the common misconception is that monetary policy is genderless. However, monetary policy can have a pronounced gender effect (see Elson, Chapter 2 in this volume). Raising real interest rates to prevent inflation can create unemployment, which may affect women quicker and for longer than it would men. Women are generally the first to be fired since they were the last hired. Tightened credit conditions are also inimical to fostering the economic independence of women entrepreneurs and in securing mortgages for homes.

Thus macro-economic policy measures based on models of undifferentiated household, undifferentiated labour supply, low productivity of women and non-discrimination may be inappropriate for fostering women's social and economic advancement. The current emphasis on restrictive fiscal and monetary policy, deregulation and privatization can impose harsh burdens on women. Decreased government regulation implicit in free-trade agreements are inimical to the environment and women's health and safety, both on the job and in society in general.

In a climate of economic recession and stagnation there are bound to be crucial battle-lines drawn in respect of the role of the state and governmental decisions to stimulate economic rebound: investment, regulation, labour-market polices, and trade policies. In such a process, there are losers and gainers. Women have a vested interest in decisions that affect the standard of living; hence they must play a key role in decisions affecting output, household income and consumption. Since women are subsidizing the economy, they must assert their right to a share in the gains of the economy.

Towards an Alternative Framework for Analysing Gender and Economic Policy

The success or failure of women's struggle to ensure economic empowerment in this era of structural change and adjustment depends on the ability to critique standard economic analysis successfully; to build a systematic and analytical basis that anchors women's claims on the economy; and to build policy mechanisms and instruments that foster economic and social advancement. The basic features of an Alternative Framework are as follows:

- The premise that economic policies do not have a benign effect on women. This requires systematic assessment of research on the impact of structural adjustment in the LDCs, where the depressing response of policy to economic conditions is the most dramatic; of the post-Reagan analysis documenting the negative impact of that policy on women in America; of Thatcherism in the United Kingdom; and of the pernicious negative effect on Canadian women of the US–Canada Free Trade Agreement.[16]

- The need to identify the 'bigger barriers' to women's economic and social advancement. These include the economic subordination of women: discrimination in the labour market, job discrimination, unpaid work, lack of recognition by policy-makers that the provision of day-care services is a crucial infrastructure and hence should be a necessary part of government investment in infrastructural expenditures. Productivity issues must be re-examined from the perspective of the gender gap.[17]

- Recognition of the fundamental restructuring of the international and domestic economy and the attendant shift in economic policies to stabilize and structurally adjust national economies. What role does women's labour play and what are the socio-economic impacts on women?

- A critical analysis of the recent trends towards political and economic liberalization and privatization; consideration of their implications for women relative to men.

- An analysis of the changing role of the state as economic actor and policy-maker and the effect of this on women relative to men.

- A people/woman-centred approach to economic development and restructuring.

- The construction of alternative indicators and statistics (both quantitative and qualitative) to account for women's participation in and contribution to the economy.[18]

Notes

1. The term 'structural adjustment' is most closely associated with the IMF and World Bank approach to resolving developing countries' external debt. The specific mechanisms include devaluation of the exchange rate, export promotion, reduction in government expenditure, and so on. However, structural adjustment is not limited to the developing countries. The Commonwealth Secretariat's report, *Engendering Adjustment*, points out that structural adjustment involves the 're-allocation of resources from one part of the economy to another, the redeployment of labour, and the creation of new skills to participate in new opportunities'. It is clear that just such a process, though differently fashioned, is underway in many advanced developed countries, most notably the US, Canada and Great Britain.

2. I am well aware that in certain OECD countries (most notably the US and the UK) there is an ongoing preoccupation with lagging productivity growth. But even in these countries women are working more hours and with more capital than before. Therefore, in a sense, the increased participation of women is a vital factor in maintaining and stabilizing productivity. Coupled with the vast contribution of female labour in the export-processing zones of the developing countries, the increased labour-market effort of women worldwide makes for a dramatic contribution to global productivity.

3. Illich develops an interesting thesis of how economic growth thrives on the exploitation of economic sex.

4. See Beneria, 1991 for a discussion of the progress in accounting for women's work.

5. Rosen points out that productivity captures the relationship between output and input. This is different from productivity improvement, which is more concerned with raising the level of productivity (see note 7 below).

6. This is the simplest measure. It reflects changes in three things: the efficiency with which labour and capital are used, the amount of tangible capital employed with each hour of labour and the average quality of labour. For a more in-depth discussion, see Fabricant, 1969.

7. According to Chinloy, 'Labor productivity growth is expressed as the sum of three components in competitive equilibrium: total factor productivity, the growth of labor quality weighted by the share of labor and the growth of capital intensity weighted by the share of capital' (Chinloy, 1981: 5).

8. This paragraph draws on observations by Drucker, 1981: 7.

9. Conventional proxy used in national income accounts is to value govern-

ment output in terms of wages and salaries of government employment. But this is still inadequate. See Mark, 1981.

10. Services include banking, insurance, real estate and health care. There is no direct measure due to the problem of defining a unit of service. Typically productivity measurers rely on substitute indicators such as consumer price index and so on. For more in-depth discussion on this, see Miller, 1978: 4–6

11. I am using the term productivity in its loose sense, in terms of women's contribution to labour power in the Millerian sense, 'that it makes people work more effectively and it contributes directly to the well being of the family, the community, the nation'. See Miller, 1978.

12. For more in-depth discussion, see Chinloy, 1981: chs. 2–5.

13. For alternative explanations of the nature and causes of the productivity slow-down in the US, see Denison, 1979; Bailey, 1982; Darby, 1982; and Thurow, 1980.

14. Sar Levitan and Diane Werneke, in analysing the Reagan administration's supply-side attempt to stimulate productivity and economic growth through tax policy, argues that 'the "reforms" offered tax relief to high income tax payers while reduction in transfer payments left low-income individuals and families worse off' (Levitan and Werneke, 1984: 72).

15. Denison (1979) argues that there is little evidence to support declining capital intensity. See also Levitan and Werneke, 1984: 25.

16. There are numerous published reports on the effect of structural adjustment on women. For example: Antrobus, 1989; Beneria, 1991; Elson, 1987; Cohen, 1987; Sen and Grown, 1985; Vickers, 1991; and Williams, 1990.

17. See Cockburn, 1988; Illich, 1982; Lewis and Astron, 1992; Sen and Grown, 1985; Standing, 1989; and Stichter and Parpart, 1990.

18. See Beneria, 1991 among others.

References

Afshar, Haleh and Carolyne Dennis (eds) (1992) *Women and Adjustment in the Third World*, Macmillan, Basingstoke.

Antrobus, Peggy (1989) 'Gender Implications of the Development Crisis'. In Norman Girvan and George Beckford (eds) *Development in Suspense*. FES and ACE.

Bailey, M.N. (1982) 'The Productivity Slow Down by Industry'. *Brookings Papers on Economic Activity* 2: 423–54.

Beneria, Lourdes (1991) 'Accounting for Women's Work: The Progress of Two Decades'. In *World Development*, vol. 20, no. 11.

Blau, Francine and Lawrence Kahn (1992) *The Gender Earnings Gap: Some International Evidence*. Paper presented at the NBER Comparative Labor Markets Project Conference in Differences and Changes in Wage Structure. Cambridge, Mass. July.

Blinder, Allan (ed.) (1990) *Paying for Productivity*. The Brookings Institute, Washington DC.

Chinloy, Peter (1981) *Labor Productivity*. Abt Books, Cambridge, Mass.

Cockburn, Cynthia (1988) *Machinery of Dominance*. Northeastern University Press, Evanston, Ill.

Cohen, Marjorie Griffin (1987) *Free Trade and the Future of Women's Work*. Garamond Press and the Canadian Centre for Policy Alternatives, Toronto.

Commonwealth Secretariat Expert Group on Women and Structural Adjustment (1989) *Engendering Adjustment for the 1990s*. Commonwealth Secretariat, London.

Darby, M.R. (1982) 'The Price of Oil and World Inflation and Recession'. In *American Economic Review*, no. 72: 738–51.

Denison, E.F. (1979) *Accounting for Slower Economic Growth: the United States in the 1970s*. Brookings Institution, Washington DC.

Drucker, Peter (1981) 'Toward the Next Economics'. In Daniel Bell and Irving Kristol (eds) *The Crisis in Economic Theory*. Basic Books, New York.

Elson, Diane (1987) 'The Impact of Structural Adjustment on Women: Concepts and Issues'. Unpublished manuscript.

Fabricant, Solomon (1969) *Productivity*. Random House, New York.

—— (1981) 'The Productivity Issue: An Overview'. In J.A. Rosow (ed.) *Productivity and Prospects for Growth*. Van Nostrand Reinhold, New York.

Gordon, D.M. (1976) 'Capitalist Efficiency and Socialist Efficiency'. In *Monthly Review*, vol. 28, no. 3.

Illich, Ivan (1982) *Gender*. Pantheon Books, New York.

Leichter, Howard (1984) 'National Productivity: A Comparative Perspective'. In *Productivity and Public Policy*. Sage Publications, New York.

Levitan, Sar A. and Diane Werneke (1984) *Productivity: Problems, Prospects, and Policies*. Johns Hopkins University Press, Baltimore.

Lewis, Jane and Gertrude Astron (1992) 'Equality, Difference and State Welfare: Labor Market and Family Policies in Sweden'. In *Feminist Studies*, vol. 18, no. 1, Spring.

Macarov, David (1982) *Worker Productivity*. Sage Publications, New York.

Mark, Jerome A. (1981) 'Productivity Measurement'. In J.M. Rosow (ed.) *Productivity Prospects for Growth*. Van Nostrand Reinhold, New York.

Medoff, J.L. and K. Abrah (1981) 'Are Those Paid More Really More Productive? The Case of Experience'. In *Journal of Human Resources*, vol. XV, no. 12.

Miller, S.M. (1978) 'Productivity and the Paradox of Service in a Profit Economy'. In *New York Times*, 13 December: 9.

Mitchell, W. and M. Watts (1985) 'Efficiency Under Capitalist Production: A Critique and Reformulation'. In *Review of Radical Political Economists*, vol. 17, no. 1/2.

Oswald, Rudy (1981) 'Unions and Productivity'. In J.M. Rosow (ed.) *Productivity and Prospects for Growth*. Van Nostrand Reinhold, New York.

Passall, Peter (1992) 'What Counts is Productivity and Productivity'. In *New York Times*, 13 December: 1.

Rosen, E.D. (1984) 'Productivity: concepts and measurements'. In M. Holzer and S.S. Nagel (eds) *Productivity and Public Policy*. Sage Publications, New York.

Rosow, Jerome M. (ed.) (1981) 'Productivity and People'. In J.M. Rosow (ed.) *Productivity and Prospects for Growth*. Van Nostrand Reinhold, New York.

Sen, Gita and Caren Grown (1985) *Development Alternatives with Women for a New Era*, DAWN Secretariat, Bangalore.

—— (1987) *Development, Crises, and Alternative Visions.* Monthly Review Press, New York.

Standing, G. (1989) 'Global Feminization through Flexible Labor'. In *World Development*, vol. 17, no. 7.

Stichter, Sharon and J.L. Parpart (eds) (1990) *Women, Employment and the Family in the International Division of Labor.* Temple University Press, Philadelphia.

Thurow, Lester (1980) 'The Productivity Problem'. In *Technology Review*, November/December.

Ullmann, John E. (ed.) (1980) *The Improvement of Productivity.* Praeger, New York.

Vickers, Jeanne (1991) *Women and the World Economic Crisis,* Zed Books, London and New Jersey.

Williams, Marjorie W. (1990) 'The Global Economic Crisis and the Fate of Women'. In *Women, Poverty and the Economy.* World Council of Churches Publications, Washington DC.

PART II

Macro-economics, the State and the Household: Lessons from the North and South

6

Restructuring in the Fishing Industry in Atlantic Canada
Martha MacDonald

Linking the debates in the North and South

Both the North and the South have experienced profound restructuring in the last decade. Developed and developing countries perceive that they must function in a changed international economic context characterized by heightened competition, shifts in the centres of economic power, rapid technological change overcoming previous barriers of space and time and facilitating profound changes in the labour process, and increasingly independent transnational corporations. There has been an increasing emphasis on the market and a hostile climate for government regulation in many countries. National governments have deregulated and imposed fiscal restraint, while international institutions like the IMF and World Bank have imposed the policies of structural adjustment. These changes have led to a decline in the well-being of the majority of people in most countries.

In recent years a considerable amount has been written on the economic crisis, restructuring and structural adjustment, most of which fails to include gender adequately. At the same time, there is a growing body of literature that addresses these issues from a feminist perspective. The problem is that there has been a failure to incorporate the feminist analysis into the mainstream of the debates and there has not been enough linking of analysis between the North and South. These concerns motivated this case study of restructuring in the fishing industry. Hopefully, the methodologies used, the theoretical thinking that informed the research and the findings will contribute to further developing the needed linkages.

This research was undertaken in the mid-1980s with Pat Connelly, a sociologist. The project was conceived to be a gendered analysis of development, using a case study of one industry, fishing, which is very important in the Atlantic region. The goal was to re-analyse the changing political economy of that industry, taking account of gender relations and the changing role of women. The industry had been studied a great deal, both by mainstream economists and by political economists. It had gone through many rounds of restructuring in the past 150 years, affected by changes in technology, international markets and capital restructuring. It was our view that one could not begin to understand the industry dynamics unless one knew the gender dynamics in both the household and the labour process.

While the project was meant to study the dynamic changes over a long time period, fieldwork was conducted in the midst of tremendous restructuring in the 1980s and therefore considerable attention was focused on understanding that restructuring and its gendered nature. The issues in the crisis and restructuring of the fishing industry were similar to those facing many industries throughout the world, and many case studies were undertaken in the 1980s to understand industry and labour process restructuring. Much of that literature, however, has paid little attention to gender. While this case-study literature tends to be micro in its focus, the purpose is to understand the overall macro-processes of global restructuring. The case studies do more than simply evaluate impacts; they seek to understand the industry dynamics as they elucidate broader global dynamics.

Theoretical and methodological approach

The Atlantic fishing industry was studied in the context of regional underdevelopment, drawing heavily on the international development literature. The region is an export-oriented resource economy, whose exploitation has never provided a basis for self-sustaining growth. Despite the industry having one of the richest fisheries resource bases in the world, its development has failed to provide adequate incomes or to avoid regular crises of overexpansion. The industry, then, was analysed in this regional context of underdevelopment and in the context of changing international markets and government regulation. The study also drew on the literature on gender and development and gender and the labour process. At a micro-level, the focus was on gender processes in the household in terms of the division of labour and allocation of labour (across paid and unpaid activities) and the gendered industry labour process – from harvesting to processing to distribution. These aspects had been ignored in the existing political economy and main-stream economic analysis of the fishery.

The theoretical approach was based on socialist feminism, which focuses on the way gender, class and race structures are interconnected and are integral to an understanding of economic reality. A major contribution of feminism is the redefinition of the concept of work to include productive labour and reproductive labour, making visible women's unrecognized labour. This approach also rejects distinctions such as those between subsistence and market sectors, informal and formal sectors, public and private spheres, in favour of a holistic view within which these aspects shape one another as they intersect and interrelate in any given society. These dichotomies have created false distinctions and have contributed to making women's involvement in the development process invisible. Socialist feminism emphasizes the inherent gender content of concepts such as economic activity, globalization and informal sector.

The analysis of the recent crisis and restructuring of the fishery also drew on the wide-ranging theoretical and empirical literature which exists under the rubric of post-Fordism, regulation theory, or flexible specialization. There are significant differences amongst these three conceptualizations, though they share many common concerns and concepts (Hirst and Zeitlin, 1991). Post-Fordism and regulation theory are rooted in a Marxist tradition, while flexible specialization draws on an institutional tradition, particularly in economics. They have in common a focus on the international reorganization of production, particularly manufacturing, and the upheaval in both micro- and macro-levels of regulatory frameworks. At the micro-level, the focus is on changes in industrial organization and the strategic possibilities and responses of firms. At the macro-level, attention is paid to the future of Keynesian policies, industrial policy and issues of international trade and financial management. One is hard-pressed to engage in discussions of crisis, globalization or international restructuring without recourse to one or more of these theoretical approaches.

These approaches, however, have been strongly criticized for their inattention to gender (Pollert, 1988; Jenson, 1989; Walby, 1989; MacDonald, 1991). This is important at many levels – from strategic responses of individual firms in changing their labour process, to the gendered effects and underlying assumptions about gender that shape the regulatory response. The underlying theme in the literature is the search for renewed profitability of firms and economies. The way that search gets resolved is an outcome of relations that exist between capital and labour, amongst firms (capital) and labour worldwide, and gender relations at all levels. An obvious example is the search for cheap labour as part of the search for profits, and the resultant feminization of the labour force worldwide. A less obvious example is the way that policy responses have implicit assumptions about gender roles and the way that household survival strategies will respond to the squeeze. The gendered nature of restructuring must be analysed at the level of the conception of strategies by corporations, governments and even economists, as well as at the more common level of impacts, if one wants truly to understand and influence the economy.

How can the broad analysis of restructuring be carried out in a way that takes account of gender? First, it is necessary to investigate several levels – from the household economy to the macro-economy – and to do that it is necessary to combine different methods and types of data, from primary and qualitative data to standard government-collected statistics.

Our research was based on six fishing community case studies in Nova Scotia. The decision to focus on communities – which is not the usual starting point for an industry analysis – was essential in enabling a holistic analysis of the industry which included issues of household-labour allocation, including unpaid domestic, subsistence and volunteer labour. Interactions at the community level are often crucial in determining industry dynamics and macro-policy impacts. Data collection included a household survey focusing on family work histories, conditions of work and the sexual division of labour, as well as in-depth interviews with some industry actors, including harvesters, processors, fish-plant workers, union representatives, wives of fishers, government regulators. Discussions were held with women in the communities singly and in groups. Oral histories were also collected in the communities. These primary data-collection techniques were combined with more standard archival research and other secondary data, including government-collected industry, census, and labour-force data.[1]

Although feminist analysis such as this often starts at the level of the household, the analysis is by no means confined to the domestic sphere or the labour sphere. The objective is to analyse an economic issue by seeing gender relations in households as one of the key analytical elements, not to begin and end at the level of the household. This fishery case study shows how including gender and household as a focus facilitates a clearer understanding of changes in the labour process and of the transformation in the industry. The household plays a crucial role in the interrelationships between the harvesting and processing sectors of the industry.[2] This research began with a simple question, 'Who works at the fish plant?' It then proceeded to study the changing patterns of household labour allocation. The premise was that one could not begin to understand the industry dynamics between harvesters and processors and between large and small capital unless one knew the gender/household dynamics and labour allocation. The bargaining power of a fisher may depend on whether or not his wife works in the fish plant, and vice versa. Household strategies shape and constrain the strategies of capital as well as being affected by capital (MacDonald and Connelly, 1989).

To return to research questions/methods, then, a gendered analysis means collecting data on many different levels. At the level of the household the crucial questions have to do with the gendered division of labour (paid and unpaid) and household labour allocation (and what that tells us about the political economy of the community, industry, region, as the case may be), and the intra-household allocation of resources. The micro-level also involves a gendered analysis of the labour process in firms, or in agriculture, or in the informal sector – wherever productive labour is undertaken. What changes are occurring at this micro-level that can be related to changes in the market or in policy? This research, for example, demonstrated that state policy relating to the fishery is based on implicit assumptions about gender relations, and that supposedly gender-neutral policies, related to licences and quotas, have very definite gender impacts (Connelly and MacDonald, 1992). One asks questions such as: Is the workload of women increasing? How do households respond to price changes of important consumer items? How have working conditions altered? How has access to and control over resources changed? How are the changes at this level related to the strategies of corporations, institutions like the IMF and GATT, and the local state?

Questions at more macro-levels of analysis also have to be rethought from a gender perspective (Elson, 1991; Moser, 1989). For example, using family-income data as an indicator of well-being becomes problematic when one is sensitized to issues of intra-family distribution of resources. Aggregate data on growth and employment can no longer be relied on as true measures of economic activity when one recognizes the importance of subsistence activities, domestic labour and the informal sector. It is also true that the status and well-being of women can decline at the same time that indicators such as income show an improvement. The fishery, like other primary sectors, has seen a rise in cash incomes and a decline in subsistence activities. How has well-being changed as a result, for women and men individually and in households? In the fishery, for example, increased capitalization and concentration of harvesting has meant that while incomes of fishers have gone up in the modern sector, the fishers are away from home for longer time periods, increasing the domestic workload of the women and constraining their opportunities for paid employment.

Changes in the balance of sectoral activities must be reviewed for gender implications. Who is winning? Who is losing? For example, in free trade debates there is often identification of industries expected to gain or lose, but the gender implications of this are less often drawn (Cohen, 1987). In the 1988 Canada–US free-trade debate in the Atlantic region, for example, the general position of industry representatives was that the fishery would benefit from free trade, given the obvious comparative advantage according to standard economic logic. Our research, however, drew attention to the different implications for various industry actors, including women both in their capacity as plant workers and as wives of harvesters. It was not at all clear that they would benefit.

Changes in the location of economic activity have gender effects. What kind of migration is required? What kind of labour mobility? How will families respond to these changes? This case study of fishing, for example, found that the restructuring had profoundly altered the geographic profile of the industry, breaking down the community-based nature of the fishery. It has also been found that the centralization of much of the service industry has altered a previous dynamic whereby there were service-sector employment opportunities for women in small towns which could supplement male incomes from the goods/resource sector (Economic Council of Canada, 1991). This proved to be a significant factor in understanding the restructuring of the fishery and the rural economy.

Findings

Several articles have been written from this research on the fishery, each taking one element of traditional economic/political economic analysis and showing how a gendered analysis alters and improves the picture. Highlights from two papers of particular relevance to the theme of engendering macro-economic policy reform will give a clearer idea of our findings and provide an illustration of the use of case studies. The first paper is on the recent industry/labour restructuring, and the second is on state policy.

The paper on the recent restructuring of the industry and the labour process shows its gendered nature and engages in broader debates about flexible specialization (MacDonald and Connelly, 1989). This paper addresses the complex interaction between industrial organization, the labour process and gender/household/community relations as changes occur in technology, resource supply, product markets, labour markets, and government policy. Most attention is paid to the crisis in the late 1970s and the subsequent restructuring, including the current crisis. The industry has long been dominated by large firms, who control both processing and harvesting through an integrated combination of an offshore fleet of large trawlers and large onshore processing plants. At the same time, an inshore sector dominated by small capital has persisted. The postwar history of the industry saw increasing concentration and dominance of the offshore sector, supported by government subsidy and policy. However, this has exacerbated the cyclical nature of the fishery, as the small firms are more flexible and adaptable to the ups and downs of the industry. The inshore sector is also crucial for the continued survival of many small coastal communities. In brief, throughout the 1970s and 1980s the industry went through cycles of overexpansion followed by stock and/or market collapse. In the early 1980s this led to the near bankruptcy of the large companies, but they were rescued and restructured by the government to avoid total collapse of the industry. The industry briefly revived in the mid-1980s, but has been in another prolonged crisis since 1989. Summarily, we make the following arguments.

The crisis in the fishery in the late 1970s grew out of contradictions between the organization of harvesting/processing in the Atlantic region and the nature of the resource supply, in the context of market changes. Technological change played a role in altering harvesting, processing and marketing. As in many industries, the new environment called for greater quality and diversity of products in rapidly changing markets, in conditions of increased international competition. Under these conditions, the larger firms, which mass-produced frozen fish blocks, faced bankruptcy, while smaller firms arose to fill the new market niches. We examine how both large and small capital restructured and sought flexibility in the 1980s, and we argue that despite the increased opportunities for flexible small-scale operations, there are also both market and institutional factors creating renewed concentration in the industry. The state has not been neutral in its mediation among the interest groups in the industry and has consistently facilitated the survival of the large capital sector (Connelly and MacDonald, 1992). Government played a major role in the initial restructuring of the industry in the early 1980s, enabling the large capital sector to survive.

The increased flexibility of firms in the fishing industry in relation to product markets has been achieved by a variety of strategies, including product diversification, marketing innovations, subcontracting, new relations between harvesting and processing, and new forms of corporate structure. These all have implications for the distribution of employment, the labour process and the well-being of workers, households and communities. Some strategies are directly aimed at labour. This paper uses case studies to show how the recovery of the large fish-processing firms in Atlantic Canada was achieved in the first instance by a concerted attack on labour costs, and that women workers bore the brunt of these changes. It argues that increased flexibility of capital can be consistent with increased control over workers and use of so-called Taylorist methods, especially in a secondary-labour-market situation in which inflexible labour is not an issue (as is the case in fish processing). The labour process changes in the fisheries have worsened conditions for the workforce and have had very different effects by gender. There has been increased feminization of the plant workforce, and women's jobs have been more deeply affected by labour process changes. Women's work on the line in fish plants and the introduction of computerized scales have enabled monitoring of individual productivity and the use of piece rates, which has amounted to a speed-up. Women have also been the primary victims of strategies for numerical flexibility, suffering more from the cutbacks in hours and weeks worked. The men's jobs in processing have been less affected by technological change and have benefited more from strategies of functional flexibility.

Restructuring has also seen the emergence of new household and community relationships to the industry, as the changes in harvesting interact with the changes in processing to create new labour-supply conditions. The increased flexibility of the large companies has resulted in decreased flexibility of particular households and communities. The largest company uses a flexible network of resource supply which no longer sustains the community-based nature of the fishery – they do not necessarily buy from the local inshore fleet; their offshore crews do not live in the home port; their plant workers may travel miles. The community basis of the fishery has also changed in the competitive sector. Inshore/midshore fishers from one community may spend months fishing out of a different community (due to seasonal restrictions). This has serious implications for the domestic workload and paid work opportunities of fisher's wives. Nowadays, the large fish companies are primarily processing fish caught on their own offshore fleet by men whose wives are unlikely to be either in the labour force or employed in the service sector. Increasingly, the husbands of women fish-plant workers are themselves fish-plant workers or are wage workers in other industries (MacDonald and Connelly, 1989).

Overall, there has been an increased specialization of families, fishers, plants and communities, which has increased their vulnerability to the crises which occur in the industry. It is becoming increasingly clear that what is good for the fishing industry (in terms of sales and profits) under its current organization may not be good for employment (direct and indirect) or community viability. Households and communities have lost the traditional flexibility that the fisheries had – with a range of species, activities and income packaging. The irony is that this loss of flexibility for individual workers, boats, plants and communities is partly a result of the search for flexibility by industry actors. Furthermore, these attempts to gain flexibility in response to the crisis of the early 1980s helped precipitate the current crisis.

The second paper analyses the impact of state policy on women in fishing communities (Connelly and MacDonald, 1992). It shows the gender assumptions implicit in some policies, as well as the outcomes

when supposedly gender-neutral policies are filtered through households/
household strategies. This paper examines three types of policies and
the way in which they apply to the Atlantic fisheries: subsidies to the
private sector; income maintenance of individuals (unemployment
insurance); and fishery regulatory policies. The aim is to show the per-
vasiveness of these general social and economic policies in the lives of
women and men, how women and men act and react both as individuals and as household members to the policies as they are implemented,
and how women and men are differentially affected by both policies
and household strategies.

Most of the literature on state policy in the fishery focuses on the
processing and harvesting sectors. Seldom is the family household
mentioned and rarely are gender issues mentioned. When the household is addressed it is seen as a cohesive unit with homogeneous
interests. The differential impact of policies on women's and men's work
inside and outside the household are always ignored. In this paper, we
argue that policies aimed at particular issues are, in fact, experienced
and interpreted as a whole by women and men within households.
Even though policies may not be directly aimed at the family household, it is in the household that policies come together in their effects,
and these effects are different on women and men. Policies often have
unintended consequences since, to the extent possible, households and
individual household members develop strategies to use policies in their
own interests. People respond and act to influence the direction of
change and the development of policy not just as individuals or groups
of workers, but also as household members. Household strategies have
different effects on women and men.

One example used in this paper has to do with the effects of boat-
building subsidies. In the brief boom that followed the establishment of
the 200-mile limit in 1977, the Fisheries Loan Board extended large
loans to fishers. Improved conditions in the fishery had a different
effect on women and men as family members rearranged their labour.
For example, in one community, fishers who had kept their boats
through the bad times began to earn higher incomes, as did the inshore
and offshore crew. Fish-plant wages, however, remained relatively low,
and families with both husband and wife in the plant had combined
incomes that were lower than most fishers. With the increase in fishers'
income, it no longer made economic sense for wives of fishers to work
for low wages in the plant. Under these conditions fishery households
rearranged their work patterns, but plant-worker households did not.
Fishers' wives in this community decided to return to the home even
though many of them preferred to continue earning a wage. This
decision was made in the interest of the household since, given their

husbands' income and the wage level in the plant, their full-time domestic labour would make a greater contribution than their wage labour.

With the withdrawal of fishers' wives from the plant, the owner had the option to raise wages, to substitute capital for labour, or to find a more marginalized labour supply. The latter option was taken. With the opening of a state-funded ferry service, women from a community across a small bay, who had previously had no employment opportunities, were happy to have the jobs at low wages. This example illustrates several points. First, the fisher/plant-worker household strategy involved the reallocation of women's, not men's, labour, and in some cases involved women putting the household's interests over their own interests. Second, the household's strategy overrode the needs of capital, that is, the employer's need for cheap labour. And finally, the ferry is an example of the state providing the conditions for capital accumulation through the provision of infrastructures when needed – in this case, an infrastructure which facilitated the continued pursuit of a gendered cheap-labour policy by the company.

Conclusion

This case study is one attempt to do gendered economic research where gender is integral to the analysis of supposedly neutral economic processes and policies. It is easier to assign gender analysis to a sub-component of the research, as is typically done. The tendency is to recognize that gender issues should be investigated, but that the main economic research can proceed without reference to gender. Gender becomes confined to a chapter in the book, to a separate session in a conference agenda. Women do the research on gender; men do the research on the economy.

Very often the dividing lines also fall between macro-analysis, assumed to be gender-neutral, and micro-analysis (at the level of the household, or the labour market, or the firm) where gender is a recognized variable. The dividing line between micro and macro is an artificial one, as are many of the dichotomies in economics and political economy. People's lives are not divided that way; nor is the economy in its functioning so divided. Case studies can be very useful in revealing the gender impacts and gendered assumptions of macro-level policies and can help cut across the micro/macro divide. Feminist scholars are leading the way in showing how a more inclusive economic analysis can improve our understanding of the global processes of development and change. Linking research on these issues across the North and South is a crucial step in the challenge of designing research agendas/methods which can incorporate gender into the core of the analysis and policy development.

Notes

1. We would like to thank the people in the communities we studied and the members of the research team, Joyce Conrad, Suzan Ilcan, Beth McIsaac, Kathy Moggridge and especially Daphne Tucker, for their contributions. This research was supported by Social Sciences and Humanities Research Council grants and by the Donner Canadian Foundation.

2. For example, in some communities at some times husbands fished for the companies who employed their wives in processsing, resulting in households bargaining over both the price of fish and the wage. In the rural communities, the prosperity of the harvesting sector also affects the labour supply to the processing sector.

References

Beneria, Lourdes (1981) 'Conceptualizing the Labour Force: The Underestimation of Women's Activities'. In *Journal of Development Studies*, vol. 17, no. 3: 10–28.

Beneria, Lourdes and Martha Roldan (1987) *The Crossroads of Class and Gender*. University of Chicago Press, Chicago and London.

Cohen, Marjorie Griffin (1987) *Free Trade and the Future of Women's Work*. Garamond Press and the Canadian Centre for Policy Alternatives, Toronto.

Commonwealth Secretariat Expert Group on Women and Structural Adjustment (1989) *Engendering Adjustment for the 1990s*. Commonwealth Secretariat, London.

Connelly, Patricia M. and Martha MacDonald (1983) 'Women's Work: Domestic and Wage Labour in a Nova Scotia Community'. In *Studies in Political Economy*, no. 10: 45–72.

——— (1990) *Women and the Labour Force*, Statistic Canada Focus on Canada Series, Supply and Services Canada, Ottawa.

——— (1992) 'State Policy, the Household and Women's Work in the Atlantic Fishery'. In *Journal of Canadian Studies*, vol. 26, no. 4.

Economic Council of Canada (1991) *Employment in the Service Economy*. Supply and Services Canada, Ottawa.

Elson, Diane (1989) 'How is Structural Adjustment Affecting Women?' In *Development*, no. 1: 67–74.

——— (1991) 'Gender Issues in Development Strategies'. Paper presented at the Seminar on Integration of Women into Development, Vienna, 9–11 December.

Harrison, B. and B. Bluestone (1988) *The Great U-Turn: Corporate Restructuring and the Polarization of America*. Basic Books, New York.

Hirst, Paul and Jonathan Zeitlin (1991) 'Flexible Specialization Versus Post-Fordism: Theory, Evidence and Policy Implications'. In *Economy and Society*, vol. 20, no. 1.

Jenson, Jane (1989) 'The Talents of Women, the Skills of Men: Flexible Specialization and Women'. In Stephen Wood (ed.) *The Transformation of Work?* Unwin Hyman, London.

Jenson, Jane, Elizabeth Hager and Ceallaigh Reddy (eds) (1988) *The Feminization of the Labour Force.* Oxford University Press, Oxford.

Kirby, Michael (1982) 'Navigating Troubled Waters: A New Policy for the Atlantic Fisheries'. Report of the Task Force on Atlantic Fisheries. Supply and Services, Ottawa.

MacDonald, Martha (1991) 'Post-Fordism and the Flexibility Debate'. In *Studies in Political Economy*, no. 36, Fall.

MacDonald, Martha and M. Patricia Connelly (1989) 'Class and Gender in Fishing Communities in Nova Scotia'. In *Studies in Political Economy*, no. 30, Autumn: 61–87.

——— (1990) 'From Crisis to Crisis: Restructuring and Work in the Fishing Industry in Atlantic Canada'. Paper presented at the International Labour Market Segmentation Conference, University of Notre Dame, April.

——— (1992) 'Labour, Gender and Adjustment'. Paper presented at IDRC Workshop on 'The Impact of the Changing International Context on the Caribbean Basin Countries', Mexico City, May.

Matthews, Ralph (1980) 'Class Interests and the Role of the State in the Development of Canada's East Coast Fishery'. In *Canadian Issues*, vol. 3, no. 1, Spring: 115–24.

Moser, Caroline (1989) 'Gender Planning in the Third World: Meeting Practical and Strategic Gender Needs'. In *World Development*, vol. 17, no. 11.

Piore, Michael and Charles Sabel (1984) *The Second Industrial Divide.* Basic Books, New York.

Pollert, Anna (1988a) 'Dismantling Flexibility'. In *Capital and Class*, no. 34, Spring.

——— (1988b) 'The "Flexible Firm": Fixation or Fact?' In *Work, Employment and Society*, vol. 2, no. 3, September: 281–316.

Rosenberg, Sam (1989) 'From Segmentation to Flexibility'. In *Labour and Society*, vol. 14, no. 4, October.

Standing, Guy (1989) 'Global Feminisation Through Flexible Labor'. In *World Development*, vol. 17, no. 7.

Thompson, P. (1983) *The Nature of Work – An Introduction to Debates on the Labour Process.* Macmillan, London.

Walby, Sylvia (1989) 'Flexibility and the Changing Sexual Division of Labour'. In Stephen Wood (ed.) *The Transformation of Work?* Unwin Hyman, London.

Ward, Kathryn (ed.) (1990) *Women Workers and Global Restructuring.* School of Industrial and Labour Relations, Cornell University, ILR Press, Ithaca, New York.

7

The Implications of Economic Restructuring for Women: The Canadian Situation

Marjorie Griffin Cohen

In this chapter I shalll argue that: (1) Economic restructuring is a gendered issue, not only in poorer countries which submit to structural adjustment initiatives, but also in industrialized countries like Canada. The changes that occur are pertinent to both labour-force activity and other aspects of women's social life. (2) The economic shifts occurring this time differ significantly from changes in the past, and the implications for women are distinct. (3) The Canadian labour force is not experiencing 'feminization', as a result of the drive for competitiveness in the restructuring process. (4) The restructuring that is occurring will inhibit the possibilities for equality between men and women, and is likely to increase disparities between classes of women.

Economic restructuring

Discussions of gender and economic restructuring rarely focus on what is happening in industrialized countries. 'Development' is studied as though it has gender implications only in developing, poor, or Third World nations. The effects on women of economic changes that occur in industrialized countries are generally ignored by policy-makers, and policies themselves are treated as though they were gender-neutral. This does not mean that women within these countries are immune from recognizing the gender implications of economic policy changes, but mainly that their experiences have yet to reach the consciousness of economists who pronounce on restructuring or of the politicians who bring such pronouncements into force.[1]

Within the past ten years increasing attention has been paid by feminist scholars to the effect of structural adjustment and stabilization programmes on women in poor or developing countries. These analyses have yielded very important insights not only to women in specific circumstances, but to the whole shape of global economic change and the implications this might hold for women, both in terms of how they effect change and are affected by it. There is a growing notion that while the circumstances of women in developing and developed countries are very different, there are some experiences that women share as a result of economic restructuring. While there is no consensus about the balance of negative over positive effects,[2] there is a sense that the forces of restructuring bring women's economic activities more and more into the market sphere and that this tendency encourages a 'feminization' of work. Feminization of the labour force implies, as Guy Standing has argued, that 'women are being substituted for men and many forms of work are being converted into the kinds of jobs traditionally geared to women' (Standing, 1989).

In Canada, the economic policy changes since 1984 certainly resemble strategies for adjustment initiatives in many developing countries. In developing nations these policies are usually described as following two goals: stabilization and structural adjustment (see Elson, 1989; Haddad, 1992). In Canada these terms are not used, but the policies are comparable. *Stabilization* initiatives are aimed at price-level and deficit reduction, and are achieved through both monetary and fiscal measures. Unusually high interest rates have brought down inflation from rates perceived by the federal government and the business community as excessively high, around 4.5 per cent a year when the current government came into power in 1984, to about 1 per cent now. This tight money policy has had a dramatic effect both on government deficits at all levels and on the unemployment rate. Since the cost of servicing existing debt grew enormously, there was increasing pressure on governments at the federal and provincial levels to reduce spending on social programmes. Expenditure reduction has taken several forms, including the shift of the burden of social welfare from the federal government to provincial governments; the elimination of programmes such as mothers' allowances and federal social housing projects; a reduction in old-age pensions; and reduced expenditures in real terms on health, education and welfare payments to the poorest. A focus on controlling the growing debt has also affected delivery of other types of services through privatization and deregulation of transportation, postal and communication systems. High interest rates, reduced social spending, and outright cuts to the civil service have contributed to increased unemployment.

The *structural adjustment* initiatives in Canada, as elsewhere, rely heavily on trade liberalization and export-led growth. Economic-policy objectives are justified only if they can promote international competitiveness: the increased exposure of the economy to outside influences is perceived as the economic 'shock' which the economy needs in order to become more efficient.[3] The cornerstones of economic policy to achieve these objectives are the Canada/US Free Trade Agreement, the proposed North American Free Trade Agreement, and the GATT. All kinds of economic activities which were perceived as 'market rigidities', causing high costs and hindering Canadian competitiveness, are challenged by relying on the discipline imposed by these trade agreements. Many policy mainstays of the Canadian economy, such as agricultural supply-management schemes and prohibitions on exporting unprocessed resources, could not be changed through political avenues, but they can be forced to change through trade liberalization.

In Canada, the 'expenditure-switching' policies associated with structural adjustment elsewhere, take the form of specific fiscal measures to stimulate business confidence. Business, it is assumed, will feel more confident and therefore be more willing to participate if the tax burden is shifted substantially from high-income earners to medium- and low-income earners, and from corporations to individuals and families. This has occurred in a rather dramatic way during the past eight years.[4]

Feminization of labour?

The policies of a minimalist state obviously have effects on the labour force, although the nature of these effects will not necessarily be similar wherever they occur. As mentioned above, whenever generalizations are made about the effects on women's labour-market experience, it is assumed that increased global competition will bring about a feminization of the workforce. The explanations for this rest on both demand and supply. The demand for female labour will increase with new competition from low-wage countries. This low-wage competition will be instrumental in weakening the bargaining position of labour in industrialized countries and ultimately depress wages. As low-wage employment spreads, women's employment will increase and women will be increasingly substituted for male workers. This should occur by converting men's jobs into the kinds traditionally done by women (Standing, 1989). More women will be pushed into the labour force because the policies of the minimalist state will place middle- and lower-income families in precarious economic positions and these families will require additional earners.

The argument appears logical and compelling, but clarification for specific circumstances needs to be made. It seems equally plausible to argue that intensified international competition could bring about a sufficient repression of wages in general so that the cost advantage of hiring women over men would not be sufficient to change the gender-

typing of jobs.[5] Given that most economies exhibit fairly dramatic occupational and industrial segregation by gender, the cost advantage of
hiring women rather than men in areas normally reserved for men
would need to be fairly large to change these rigidities. A shift from
male to female workers is likely to occur when export-oriented production expands rather rapidly, particularly if this is labour-intensive and
requires skills which are relatively easily acquired. It is much less likely
to happen when economic policies bring about fairly rapid increases in
unemployment and there is no significant growth in employment in
export-oriented industries. This appears to be more typical of what is
occurring in Canada.

Referring to the 'feminization' of labour in Canada as a result of
global restructuring seems inappropriate, because women have been
increasingly entering the labour force since the turn of the century.
While the labour force, until the 1970s, could not by any stretch of the
imagination be considered 'feminized' (simply because the female composition of the total labour force was very small until World War II,
and even until the 1970s most women were not engaged in paid work),
there was a fairly dramatic increase in women's labour-force participation in the postwar period. So, in this sense the workforce has become
more 'feminized' as a result of the restructuring of the economy which
has occurred over the course of the century.

However, the restructuring associated with global changes, or more
specifically that associated with the increasing mobility of international
capital and the Free Trade Agreement, may be slowing the acceleration
of women's participation in the labour force or even causing it to
decrease. In 1966 slightly over 35 per cent of adult women in Canada
were in the labour force. This increased by about 10 per cent a decade,
or 1 per cent a year, until 1988. From 1988 to 1990 the growth in
women's participation rate decelerated to about 0.5 per cent a year
(Department of Finance, 1991) (see Table 7.1). From July 1991, there
has been an absolute drop in women's participation rate from 58.6 per
cent to 57.4 per cent in the spring of 1992 (Statistics Canada). It is not
possible to know if this is a trend; but because of the extraordinary
pressures on women's work in the manufacturing sector as a result of
free trade, it certainly appears that this is more than a phenomenon
associated with a recession. In previous recession periods, the more
normal behaviour is for women increasingly to enter the labour force,
presumably because reductions in household incomes force more women
to look for work. Women now account for about 45 per cent of the
total labour force.

Male labour-force participation has remained almost static throughout the 1980s (76.6 per cent), but has dropped from a high of 79.8 per

Table 7.1 Employment in Canada (1,000s)

	1988	1991	change	% change
		Female employment		
All industries	5368.2	5588.7	220.5	4.1
Agriculture	137.4	146.2	8.8	6.4
Other primary	37.0	36.0	−1.0	−2.7
Manufacturing	600.3	533.9	−66.4	−11.1
Construction	78.9	79.6	0.7	0.9
Transport, communications & utilities	227.7	240.5	12.8	5.6
Trade	966.2	986.2	20.0	2.1
Finance, insurance & real estate	440.8	455.6	14.8	3.4
Service sector	2544.2	2746.1	201.9	7.9
Public administration	335.7	364.6	28.9	8.6
		Male employment		
All industries	6867.3	6751.4	−124.9	−1.8
Agriculture	306.4	302.0	−4.4	−1.4
Other primary	257.0	243.7	−13.3	−5.2
Manufacturing	1503.7	1330.8	−172.9	−11.5
Construction	646.8	614.9	−31.9	−4.9
Transport, communications & utilities	676.7	675.9	−0.8	−0.1
Trade	1201.3	1182.5	−18.8	−1.6
Finance, insurance & real estate	287.4	304.1	16.7	5.8
Service sector	1517.3	1630.2	112.9	7.4
Public administration	479.8	467.4	−12.4	−2.6

cent in 1966, to a low of 73.5 per cent in 1992. But it is still clear that males predominate in the labour force, accounting for about 55 per cent of all workers. However, just looking at aggregate figures about participation rates does not give a clear indication of the extent of the 'feminization' of the workforce. There is a high degree of segregation of work by gender in Canada and this does not appear to be changing significantly, either as more women enter the labour force, or as equality legislation is implemented. The evidence does not indicate that restructuring is causing women to take jobs previously held by men, or that work which was characteristically male is assuming more typically female-type forms. What is occurring is more complex.

Men's jobs do not appear to be changing character so that women can take them. Usually when men lose jobs, the jobs disappear altogether. For example, the occupations and industries with the highest unemployment rates for males are not the industries or occupations that are seeing increases in female employment. The highest average unemployment rates for males in Canada in 1991 were in forestry (26 per cent unemployed) and construction (23 per cent). There was no increase in women's employment in these industries and virtually no change in women's proportion of the total labour force in both industries between 1988 and 1991.[6] The gender-specific nature of employment appears to maintain its rigidity when unemployment rates are high; this is typical not only of sectors dominated by males. In the manufacturing sector it seems that women are not replacing men in any industries, even those where men are a small proportion of the workforce. The best example is the clothing industry, which, more than any other manufacturing industry, is 'feminized', and has been so for most of the twentieth century. Women account for 75 per cent of the labour force and are not replacing men as restructuring occurs; rather, both men and women have lost jobs. For women this is relatively more devastating because the clothing industry is the second largest employer of women in the manufacturing sector (the food and beverage industry employs more), while clothing industry jobs for men are few and relatively insignificant to total male employment in manufacturing.

Changes in women's employment

Although women are not replacing men in industries or occupations which were typically male, significant changes in women's employment are occurring. The most notable change is the intensification of non-standard forms of work in which women have typically predominated in the past, particularly part-time and temporary work. But also, in some cases, there appears to be a reversion to older forms of work organization, such as contracting-out and home-work. Even traditionally standard work for women, such as nursing, is increasingly organized through contract agency work and is more likely to take the form of temporary or part-time employment. But older forms of home-work are making a comeback. Particularly significant here are the increased employment of live-in domestic workers and work for the garment industry done in the home.

Table 7.2 Employment in Canadian manufacturing (1,000s)

	1988	1991	change	% change
All manufacturing	600.3	533.9	−66.4	−11.1
Food & beverages	85.5	80.9	−4.6	−5.4
Rubber & plastics	23	23.7	0.7	3.0
Leather	12.4	8.6	−3.8	−30.6
Textiles	23.9	21.3	−2.6	−10.9
Clothing	93.4	74.5	−18.9	−20.2
Wood	15.4	14.9	−0.5	−3.2
Furniture & fixtures	14.8	9.9	−4.9	−33.1
Paper & allied trades	18.6	18.3	−0.3	−1.6
Printing & publishing	72.1	68.2	−3.9	−5.4
Primary metal	13.8	9.8	−4.0	−29.0
Metal fabrication	23.9	23.2	−0.7	−2.9
Machinery	12.7	10.5	−2.2	−17.3
Transport equipment	47.8	48.6	0.8	1.7
Electrical products	60.8	50.5	−10.3	−16.9
Non-metal minerals	9.7	8.5	−1.2	−12.4
Chemicals and chemical products	33.4	29.1	−4.3	−12.9
Miscellaneous manufacturing	31.1	29.8	−1.3	−4.2

The manufacturing sector is the site of the most dramatic changes in women's employment. These are changes that appear to be permanent because they are associated with plant closures rather than lay-offs.[7] In the first three years of the FTA, women's employment in manufacturing decreased by over 11 per cent or 66,400 jobs. The biggest numbers of jobs lost for women were in the clothing and electrical-products industries: almost 19,000 (a 20 per cent decline) in clothing; and 10,300 (17 per cent) in electrical production. In some manufacturing industries which were not large employers of women, the decreases in percentage terms have been huge. For example, in the furniture industry 33 per cent fewer women were employed in 1991 than in 1988; in leather 31 per cent fewer; in primary metals 39 per cent (see Table 7.2).

The devastating effect of free trade on women in manufacturing is also reflected in the unemployment rate, which rose from 10.2 per cent in 1988 to 14.6 per cent in 1991. Men's unemployment in 1991 averaged 11.1 per cent, up from 6.2 per cent in 1988. Unemployment figures for women in manufacturing at this point may give a better indication of the effects of restructuring, and especially free trade, on women than

Table 7.3 Distribution of female employment by occupation

Occupation	1984	1988	1991
	% of total workforce		
Clerical	79.1	79.8	80.8
Services	55.5	57.0	56.6
Sales	42.7	45.9	46.1
Medicine & health	77.8	79.0	80.1
Teaching	58.8	62.2	64.7
Managerial, administration	31.6	36.2	40.4
Product fabricating, assembly & repair	22.9	22.5	20.4
Agriculture	25.2	25.8	27.6
Social sciences	55.2	58.4	60.1
Processing & machining	15.7	16.4	16.9
Artistic & recreation	39.0	43.8	41.9
Natural sciences	17.0	16.2	18.1
Materials handling	21.1	20.6	20.6
Other crafts & equipment operating	20.1	24.1	20.8
Transport equipment operating	6.8	7.8	8.7
Religion	15.6	18.8	22.1
Forestry, logging, fishing, hunting	—	—	—
Mining and quarrying	—	—	—
	% of female workforce		
Clerical	32.1	30.8	29.3
Services	17.9	17.0	16.6
Sales	9.6	10.0	9.8
Medicine & health	9.1	9.0	9.7
Teaching	6.0	6.1	6.5
Managerial, administration	8.0	10.4	12.0
Product fabricating, assembly & repair	4.7	4.2	3.4
Agriculture	2.7	2.2	2.3
Social sciences	2.2	2.3	2.8
Processing & machining	2.0	1.8	1.6
Artistic & recreation	1.5	1.8	1.7
Natural sciences	1.4	1.3	1.6
Materials handling	1.2	1.1	0.9
Other craft & equipment operating	0.6	0.7	0.5
Transport equipment operating	0.6	0.7	0.7
Construction trades	0.2	0.3	0.3
Religion	0.1	0.1	0.1
Forestry, logging, fishing, hunting	—	—	—
Mining & quarrying	—	—	—

Source: Statistics Canada, unpublished data, ref. MR92010

unemployment statistics are likely to reveal at a later date. This is assuming that the job loss for women in manufacturing is likely to be permanent and women will increasingly drop out of the manufacturing labour force.[8]

More women working for pay has meant the intensification of the feminized character of occupations which have always been important for women: teaching, nursing, clerical, and service work. But in almost all occupational categories women have assumed a slightly larger proportion of the workforce[9] (see Table 7.3). Generally the changes have been small except in the category of managerial and administrative jobs. Women now hold over 40 per cent of all managerial and administrative positions, which represents a substantial increase from 1984 when they held 31 per cent. With these jobs now accounting for about 12 per cent of total female employment, and being the third most important occupational category for women, this would seem to be a significant change in a fairly short period of time (see Table 7.3). It would also appear to indicate both a feminization of a traditionally male field and a substantial reduction in the sex segregation of the workforce.

Appearances here are quite deceiving, however, since the changes are more likely the result of new occupational definitions instituted in 1984 than genuine increases of women in managerial and administrative positions (Shea, 1990). The percentage decreases in women's occupational distribution in clerical and service occupations seem to mirror their proportional increases in managerial and administrative jobs. The likelihood that some clerical and service jobs have been reclassified as managerial or administrative is further strengthened by comparing wage data changes from 1984 to 1990. The wage gap between men and women in these occupations has widened substantially. For full-time/full-year work, women earned, on average, 63.3 per cent of what men did in 1984. This figure dropped to 60.9 per cent in 1990 (see Table 7.4). Total average earnings for all women workers in this occupational category dropped from 59.2 per cent of men's earnings to 57.6 per cent. By 1990 more than 35 per cent of women classified as having managerial/administrative jobs earned less than $20,000 a year, and the vast majority (65 per cent) earned less than $30,000 a year. In contrast, 72 per cent of males in this category earned more than $30,000 a year, with 36 per cent earning more than $50,000 (Statistics Canada, 1992). All this would indicate that women's work as managers and administrators is less highly valued than men's, and has become less valuable over the past six years. It is estimated that about 40 per cent of the change in the proportion of women managers and administrators is a result of a renaming of clerical work (Shea, 1990).

The increases in managerial and administrative work for women,

Table 7.4 Earnings gap 1981–90 (female wages as % of male wages)

Occupation	1981	1984	1988	1990
Manager/administrative				
average earnings	55.3	59.2	59.3	57.6
full-time/full-year	57.9	63.3	62.1	60.9
Clerical				
average earnings	62.1	64.7	71.2	69.7
full-time/full-year	66.7	67.9	73.4	72.7
Services				
average earnings	49.3	50.3	50.8	55.3
full-time/full-year	57.4	54.6	57.1	61.1
Teaching				
average earnings	62.4	65.6	69.1	69.0
full-time/full-year	76.5	74.8	79.6	76.2
Processing				
average earnings	49.0	39.7	53.8	49.9
full-time/full year	54.6	63.8	58.8	58.6
Sales				
average earnings	48.1	49.4	49.3	50.6
full-time/full-year	59.6	54.6	56.5	60.2
Fabricating/assembly				
average earnings	53.5	53.8	52.6	57.1
full-time/full-year	56.8	56.3	56.2	60.2
Medical and health				
average earnings	45.0	49.8	49.3	51.7
full-time/full-year	50.8	54.9	54.1	58.5

Source: Calculated from Statistics Canada, 1992.

while not as impressive as the statistics indicate at first glance, are not insignificant, however. Rather, these changes indicate a growing dissimilarity in women's work circumstances. While women's work before the 1980s was primarily confined to low-wage work, there appears to be a growing polarization in women's work. The polarization in the workforce is frequently associated with the decrease in manufacturing jobs, which were more likely to be unionized and high-waged, and the increase in service-sector work (Economic Council of Canada, 1990: 15). While this structural shift may be a factor in a polarization in men's wages, this is unlikely to be a factor in the polarization in women's wages. This is primarily because women's wages in manufacturing occu-

Table 7.5 Part-time employment 1984–88 (% of total employment)

	1991	1988	1984
All industries	16.4	15.4	15.3
Males			
all ages	8.1	7.6	7.6
15–24	33.3	29.1	26.8
25+	3.9	2.9	3.1
Females			
all ages	25.6	25.2	25.6
15–24	43.4	37.3	35.0
25+	21.4	22.0	22.7

Source: Statistics Canada, unpublished data, reference numbers SOC61, SIC61.

pations were lower than in most other occuptions for women. For example, women in processing occupations earned, on average, for full-time/full-year work 16 per cent less than the average woman clerical worker, 35 per cent less than the average woman health-care worker, 45 per cent less than the average woman teacher and only 10 per cent more than the average woman service industries worker (calculated from Statistics Canada, 1992).

The structural shifts, or changes in the industrial and occupational composition of jobs, are probably less significant for increasing differences between women than the restructuring of jobs within industries.[10] The most dramatic changes appear to be related to age differences. The growth in non-standard work for young women has been fairly dramatic, so that in 1991 over 43 per cent of all young women in the labour force did not have full-time jobs (see Table 7.5). What appears most telling is the shift in the wage differentials between younger and older working women during the 1980s, with younger women receiving substantially less, relatively, and older workers receiving slightly more (Myles, 1992: 356) – a trend that appears to be affecting all occupations and all industries. It is receiving relatively less attention than shifts away from manufacturing jobs, primarily because it is affecting young women who, it is assumed, will improve their employment circumstances as they remain longer in the workforce. However, the dramatic decrease in the relative wages of young workers and the increasing prevalence of two-tiered wage systems indicate that something more long-lasting may be at work. Many trade unions, for example, sense that the wage differentials for new labour-force entrants is an indication of a general wage restructuring, but one which will take its time to affect older workers with seniority.[11]

The overall wage gap between men and women for full-time/full-year work appears to have narrowed slightly, although Canada still has the highest difference of any modern industrialized country. Generally, when comparisons between men's and women's wages have been made, very careful attention has been given to comparing like situations. Because full-time/full-year work is more standard for men, that measure has been used for comparisons between men's and women's wage rates. However, this type of comparison may be less appropriate as standard types of work become even more elusive for women. Also, money earnings themselves are not the only indication of a narrowing or widening of the wage gap between men and women. Two-tiered compensation packages often reduce fringe benefits, and benefits such as pensions are totally absent from compensation for many forms of women's labour. As women's labour increasingly takes a non-standard form, these types of issues will need to be examined when comparisons between men's and women's wages are made. It is likely that the slight narrowing of the money wage gap may be insignificant in comparison with total compensation.

Conclusion

The gendered effects of economic restructuring will take different forms in different countries. Because women in all countries receive substantially less money for their work than do men, it is often assumed that the increased competition which is brought about by trade liberalization and export-led growth policies will encourage a feminization of labour throughout the world. This has not occurred in Canada because widespread unemployment, as a result of the structural adjustment initiatives, has brought about general downward pressures on wages. The gendered rigidities in the labour market have been maintained, and in typically feminized industries have increased. The major changes in women's employment appear to be in the acceleration of non-standard forms of work and a reduction in their labour-force participation rate.

Economic adjustment policies in Canada have proceeded without much regard for their impact on labour. Initially when there was some question about Canada supporting the Canada/US Free Trade Agreement, the government made considerable efforts to discuss what types of labour adjustment programmes could be put into place. Women's groups and trade unions were convinced that the impact on jobs would be severe and would be felt immediately. While the government tried to dismiss these fears, it is now clear that they were reasonable ones.

Notes

1. The impact of macro-economic policy on women is rarely discussed in developed countries. Economic issues for the most part have been confined to micro-economic levels, focusing on matters of pay, time, work concentration, and job segregation.

2. While on balance the impact of global restructuring is seen as having a negative effect on women, there is extreme caution about pronouncing and making generalizations for all women. See, for example, Lim, 1983.

3. Much has been written on this in Canada as a justification for free trade. See, for example, Lipsey and Smith, 1985; Crispo, 1988.

4. The effect, unfortunately, has not been as stimulative to economic performance and business 'confidence' as was hoped. For an analysis of tax changes, see Brooks, 1992.

5. For example, Cagatay and Berik (1990) argue that re-regulation and repression of labour in Turkey has brought about labour-cost competitiveness. As a result, a feminization of the standard labour force has not occurred. See Chapter 9.

6. Women comprise 11 per cent of the forestry industry and 10 per cent of the construction industry employment; they are mainly employed in clerical jobs.

7. In Ontario, which accounts for over one-half of all female manufacturing employment in Canada, 65 per cent of the job losses during the past three years have been a result of permanent plant closures. This is in dramatic contrast with Ontario plant closures in the 1982 recession, which accounted for 22 per cent of job losses (Campbell, 1992).

8. Women's unemployment rate was higher than men's in eight of the past twelve years. Generally, overall unemployment rates for men and women are not too dissimilar.

9. The occupations where women as a proportion of the total have decreased slightly are product fabricating, assembling and repairing, and materials handling (Statistics Canada).

10. Gordon Becherman (1992) makes this point for the labour force as a whole.

11. For example, different working conditions and wage scales for new workers have been vigorously contested by unions, but ultimately instituted in the airline industries and in fish-processing plants.

References

Becherman, Gordon (1992) 'The Disappearing Middle'. In Daniel Drache (ed.) *Getting on Track: Social Democratic Strategies for Ontario*. McGill-Queen's University Press, Montreal.

Brooks, Neil (1992) *Paying for Civilized Society: The Need for Fair and Responsible Tax Reform*. Canadian Centre for Policy Alternatives, Ottawa.

Cagatay, Nilufer and Gunseli Berik (1990) 'Transition to Export-Led Growth in Turkey: Is There a Feminization of Employment'. In *Review of Radical Economics*, vol. 22, no. 1: 115–34.

Campbell, Bruce (1992) 'Canada Under Siege: Three Years into the Free Trade Era'. Canadian Centre for Policy Alternatives, Ottawa.

Crispo, John (ed.) (1988) *Free Trade: The Real Story*. Gage, Toronto.

Department of Finance (1991) *Quarterly Economic Review: Annual Reference Tables*, June.

Economic Council of Canada (1990) *Good Jobs, Bad Jobs: Employment in the Service Economy*. Ottawa.

Elson, Diane (1989) 'The Impact of Structural Adjustment on Women: Concepts and Issues'. In B. Onimode (ed.) *The IMF, the World Bank and the African Debt*, vol. 2. Zed Books, London.

Haddad, Lawrence (1992) 'Gender and Adjustment: Theory and Evidence to Date'. Paper presented at the workshop on The Effects of Policies and Programs on Women, International Food Policy Research Institute, January.

Lim, Linda Y.C. (1983) 'Capitalism, Imperialism, and Patriarchy: The Dilemma of Third World Women's Work in Multinational Factories'. In June Nash and Maria Patricia Fernandez-Kelly (eds) *Women, Men and the International Division of Labour*, SUNY Press, Albany.

Lipsey, Richard G. and Murray G. Smith (1985) *Taking the Initiative: Canada's Trade Options in a Turbulent World*. C.D. Howe Institute, Toronto.

Myles, John (1992) 'Post-Industrialism and the Service Economy'. In Daniel Drache and Meric Gertler (eds) *The New Era of Global Competition*. McGill–Queen's University Press, Montreal.

Shea, Catherine (1990) 'Changes in Women's Occupations'. Social Trends Statistics Canada, Ottawa, Autumn.

Standing, Guy (1989) 'Global Feminization through Flexible Labor'. In *World Development*, vol. 17, no. 7: 1077–95.

Statistics Canada (n.d.) *The Labour Force*, Catalogue 71-001, selected years.

Statistics Canada (1992a) 'Labour Force Annual Averages, 1981–1991', Catalogue 71–529.

Statistics Canada (1992b) *Earnings of Men and Women*, Catalogue 13–217, Ottawa.

8

Gender Bias and Macro-economic Policy: Methodological Comments from the Indonesian Example

Barbara Evers

World Bank structural adjustment and International Monetary Fund stabilization programmes have greatly influenced the shaping of the global macro-economic policy environment of the 1980s and 1990s, particularly, though not exclusively, in developing countries. Structural adjustment and stabilization policies are the product of neo-classical economic thinking, which emphasizes the superiority of competition in 'free markets' and the central role of private economic decision-makers (investors, producers and consumers) in shaping economic life. Central to the macro-economic orthodoxy of the 1980s is the reduction in state economic activities, both with respect to the size and scope of the bureaucracy as well as to the state's retreat from productive activities through privatization of state assets. The chapters in Part I of this volume establish the analytical importance of taking account of the influence of gender on the outcome of such policies. The purpose of this chapter is to consider how to evaluate the differential impact of macro-economic policies with regard to gender. The following comments are essentially illustrative and arise from recent research in Indonesia which is concerned with evaluating changes in the demand for labour in the manufacturing sector during the period of stabilization and structural adjustment in the 1980s (Evers, 1992).[1]

The link between macro-economic policies and meso- or micro-economic categories such as the household or gender is neither an obvious nor an easy relationship to formalize. Although orthodox economic theory does not incorporate 'micro' concepts such as gender into the broader 'macro' picture, conceptually there is a clear link between the different levels of economic activity. Indeed, this is an area of study with a growing body of empirical and theoretical literature (reviewed by Bakker in Chapter 1 of this volume; see for example, Afshar and Dennis, 1992; Elson, 1991). The rest of this chapter discusses some of the analytical considerations in developing a methodology for evaluating the gender dynamics of macro-economic policy measures. Much of this discussion draws on methodologies that economists have used in adjustment-impact studies which have focused on the various outcomes of restructuring with respect to the agricultural sector, poverty, investment, growth, productivity and the balance of payments.

Distinguishing between stabilization and structural adjustment

Although in practice the policies of structural adjustment and stabilization overlap, they are conceptually distinct. The dynamics of demand-oriented policies will differ from those of supply-oriented reforms, although the relationship between them may be mutually reinforcing or contradictory. If one evaluates the effects of reforms with the aim of improving policy design, then one must be able to demonstrate the processes by which particular policies (or combinations of policies) bring about any given outcome. For example, research suggests that women are disproportionately disadvantaged by the effects of restructuring under stabilization and structural adjustment. One of the processes by which women are disadvantaged is through the way in which cuts in government expenditure (demand-reducing policies) affect the 'production and reproduction of human beings' within the household (see, for example, Elson, 1989). Women's relation to the goods and services provided by the state is linked to their role within the household. As key consumers of public services (education and health care), as well as goods and services that are subsidized by the government (basic foodstuffs, electricity, public transport), any changes in the conditions under which these goods and services are supplied will impinge on those primarily responsible for the welfare of the household, normally women. At the same time, micro-level research has pointed to the strong linkages between female welfare, child mortality and literacy rates and the general incidence of poverty.

When the state withdraws from certain activities, as the economy 'adjusts' the market should, in theory, fill the gap. However, resources are not attracted to the activities of production and reproduction within the household; rather, resources are encouraged to switch into tradeable activities and out of non-tradeables. What happens to the relative position of women and men in this process, and how do their gender roles interact with the need for flexibility in the transfer of labour from one activity to another? To explain the dynamics of resource-switching under adjustment one must also refer to the gender division of labour within the household. If, as has been argued, structural adjustment is associated with the 'feminization' (see Standing, 1989) of certain sectors of the labour force, what happens to women's responsibilities within the household? In certain countries and in certain sectors, structural adjustment has encouraged the rapid growth of low-paid, labour-intensive, female employment in export-processing zones (for example, Malaysia, Indonesia, Sri Lanka, Mexico) in the electronics, footwear and clothing industries, but women may also be displaced as workers during the process of adjustment. In practice, the changes that occur in an adjusting economy depend on a number of factors: initial conditions in the adjusting economy; the prevailing economic climate; the nature of the gender division of labour; the particular technical change occurring within an industry; the nature of sectoral change within the economy – any of which may discourage the employment of women in preference to men, and female employment participation rates, on average, may actually worsen (see Cagatay, Chapter 9 in this volume). One cannot predict, *prima facie*, what the gender implications of adjustment will be. This will depend on a number of factors, some of which are considered below.

The national economy in a global context

As national economies become more open to external influences and become more export-oriented, international factors will assume greater and more direct significance in national economic life. The outcome of adjustment will depend partially on the global and regional environment in which the reforms take place. The rate of growth in international economic variables will be a significant factor in the way a country experiences adjustment. Clearly, the slower the rate of growth of foreign investment and the more limited the international supply of credit, the more risky it is for an economy to shift to an export-oriented industrialization strategy (see Page, 1991). With respect to the external economic environment, regional economic factors are also important. The relative growth in investment and exports of manufactures from South-east Asian economies may be contrasted with those of sub-Saharan Africa; and, in turn, the relative effects of adjustment on women in the two regions may be examined. To compensate for the slow growth worldwide in direct foreign investment and in world trade, the relative dynamism of other Asian economies has been a factor in the Indonesian experience of adjustment that many consider to have been 'successful' (see Thorbecke, 1992). In particular, Indonesia has benefited from rapidly growing investment from Asian newly industrializing countries (NICs) such as South Korea and Taiwan, which have moved their more labour-intensive industries to countries with lower labour costs (Thee, 1991).

The national economy

The influence of the macro-economic environment – for example, the rates of growth of gross domestic product (GDP), investment and government expenditure – will have a bearing on the outcome of adjustment policies. Women may benefit from the temporary suspension of certain forms of discrimination when the economy is growing rapidly and demand for labour is strong, but not during periods of stagnation or decline (for example, the employment of women in Western capitalist countries in non-traditional occupations during periods of war when the supply of male labour was limited, and the retrenchment of women workers when men returned from the war). Following a burst of economic activity in the late 1980s, the growth of the Indonesian economy slowed down in the early 1990s, and investment in certain labour-intensive industries (some of which tend to be large employers of women) has slowed and in some cases declined very rapidly (Manning, 1992); this will have a bearing on the way adjustment proceeds.

Indeed, past rates of economic growth, as well as the general level of GDP per capita and the distribution of income, will influence the way in which adjustment and stabilization policies interact with existing conditions. In general, adjustment programmes have not had a positive impact on poverty alleviation, although the Indonesian example is said to be one of the exceptions (Thorbecke, 1992). One explanation for Indonesia's relative success with adjustment is the pre-reform period of relatively strong and sustained growth. The conditions which prevailed in the period before the decline in oil revenues prompted the need for adjustment, providing fertile ground for a positive response to the adjustment reforms with regard to poverty alleviation and further growth in the economy (Huppi and Ravallion, 1991). The relative size and dynamism of the three main sectors of the economy – agriculture, manufacturing and services – is a significant factor to take into account when evaluating the impact of adjustment policies. We may find that economies with a very small manufacturing sector fare less well (under certain circumstances) than those with a relatively large and sophisticated manufacturing base. Structural adjustment in sub-Saharan Africa, where many countries have a relatively small manufacturing sector and agriculture and mining are dominant sectors, has not been accompanied by the growth in foreign investment experienced by some Asian countries. Nor do we see in sub-Saharan Africa a significant trend of growing female employment in labour-intensive manufactures, as experienced by other developing countries. The dynamics of change in the agricultural sector will reveal important information on the gender implications of adjustment in largely agrarian societies, particularly where women-headed households constitute a significant share of the total. A sectoral profile of the role of women in the economy can assist in highlighting the most important sectoral areas for intervention to affect the relative status of women.

Industry/sub-sectoral considerations

Capital-intensive versus labour-intensive industries   During the process of adjustment, assuming all other factors remain unchanged, the relative price of capital rises with higher interest rates and more expensive imports of machinery; and the relative price of labour declines through devaluation and 'liberalization' of labour markets. In response to changes in relative prices, labour-intensive industries are expected to grow faster than capital-intensive ones. Theoretically, this should correspond with growth in tradeable in relation to non-tradeable industries. The evaluation of the gender impact of macro-economic reform should take account of how the gender division of labour maps onto the sub-sectoral divisions in the economy: between labour-intensive and capital-intensive subsectors and between tradeables and non-tradeables.[2]

Traditionally, capital-intensive subsectors are heavy industries, usually protected by the state. The classic labour-intensive sub-sectors include textiles, food and beverages, furniture making, and so on. In practice, however, it is difficult to divide sectors in this way. For example, within the textiles industry, weaving and spinning are relatively capital-intensive subsectors, while clothing manufacture is labour-intensive. In the automotive and electronics industry, component making is capital-intensive but assembly is labour-intensive.

Tradeables versus non-tradeables   At the same time, policies aim to stimulate the production of tradeables over non-tradeables. The classic tradeable goods for adjusting economies are labour-intensive manufactures: clothing, furniture, processed food, component assembly in electronics and automobile industries. Tradeables can also include capital-intensive industries like petroleum and mining and efficient import substitutes. Non-tradeables are goods which could not be traded on world markets either for reasons of price, quality or the intrinsic nature of the good or service – this includes social services such as nursing, teaching, child-care provision.

The enterprise

At the level of the enterprise, changes in relative prices (that is, a relative rise in the cost of capital and a decline in the cost of labour) should, in theory, stimulate changes in techniques of production. Capital-intensive techniques should be scrapped in favour of more labour-intensive ones. However, the experience of some countries suggests that the opposite is true. In the absence of import controls, trade liberalization may tend to increase the capital-intensity of industries that were previously unable to import. In such cases, the trade-liberalizing effects will be stronger than the relative price effects of adjustment. In more open economies, the ability and, indeed, the need to compete on foreign markets often stimulates producers to use the most up-to-date technology affordable. If markets are growing, the relatively high price of capital may be of secondary importance to the survival of the firm, particularly if labour costs are very low.

The textile industry in Indonesia provides a good example of the differential effects of adjustment policies, at both the industry or sectoral level and the enterprise level. Adjustment is associated with the takeoff in clothing manufacture, which is a highly labour-intensive process and one where the vast majority of workers are young women. At the same time, production of cloth and thread has also increased (though more slowly). These industries are relatively capital-intensive. Cloth can be produced by both hand looms and more productive mechanical looms. Although the change in relative prices should, in theory, encourage producers to use more labour-intensive techniques of production (where the relative demand for female labour is high), the forces of competition and the nature of world markets create a different set of incentives. In order to compete on world markets, producers may respond by upgrading their techniques of production and using more capital-intensive techniques, that is, more sophisticated mechanical looms. While the traditional sector continues to specialize in hand-loom weaving (which is traditionally a female occupation), the modern sector is re-placing hand looms with power looms, where the sex of the operator has become less relevant. Thus at the industry level (textiles) two forces are at work during the adjustment process: first, the increased demand for female labour in the labour-intensive clothing industry; and, second, the displacement of female-operated hand looms by power looms. Employment per loom has declined rapidly with higher productivity and with the change in technology; the propensity to employ women as weavers has also declined. Thus the dynamics of changing incentives under adjustment, coupled with the forces of competition encouraged by trade liberalization, have stimulated contradictory dynamics within the labour market (Evers, 1992).

At the enterprise and market (meso) levels, the effects of rising imports as a result of trade liberalization have been given little consideration, as most of the literature focuses on the balance-of-payments effects of trade liberalization. As explained above, the introduction of new machine-intensive production may have actually changed the sexual division of labour. One may find that women are displaced from traditionally female jobs when new and more productive machinery is introduced.

On the meso-level, the trade-liberalization aspect of adjustment can alter market conditions of supply to the enterprise, so that international markets are favoured over local markets. In the case of Indonesia, there is anecdotal evidence to suggest that local producers who supply inputs to the domestic market experience difficulty in obtaining supplies of raw materials because their orders are smaller and more frequent than those of exporters. If marketing of inputs is reoriented towards the larger and often metropolitan producer, then small, geographically scattered producers may experience greater difficulties associated with the reorientation of the economy towards export markets. Referring back to the textile example, most hand-loom production is undertaken on a relatively small scale; thus the changes in the structure of distribution disadvantage hand-loom producers relative to large weavers using power looms. In effect, industries where female employment is most concentrated is disadvantaged relative to those where it is less concentrated. Thus, the mapping of the sexual division of labour onto the size and market orientation of a firm is highly relevant. For instance, where international institutions selectively intervene in economies to promote women's employment projects, one may find that the macro-economic environment is counterproductive and as such will have a bearing on the success or failure of such projects.

Another issue to consider at the enterprise level is the organization of production. There is some evidence, for example, that subcontracting increases under structural adjustment, and in general the implications of 'flexibility' of labour are important in the adjustment scenario. This issue has been addressed in some detail by the International Labour Office (see International Labour Office, 1989). Certainly there was evidence of extensive subcontracting arrangements in the rattan and clothing industries in Indonesia (Berry, forthcoming) but there is no clear indication of a trend. One can say, however, that growth of industries where subcontracting is an important aspect of the production process will tend to raise the incidence of subcontracting, even if the tendency for certain industries to subcontract does not increase.

National-level regional dynamics of adjustment

Structural adjustment is likely to introduce new regional dynamics into an economy. The switching of resources from one sector to another often corresponds to the physical movement of labour and increased

interregional capital mobility. In Indonesia, for example, most new investment in textiles and clothing is concentrated in two metropolitan areas
in West Java, in Bandung and Jakarta. Labour is supplied from a far
wider area, creating new migration and urbanization dynamics.
MacDonald (see Chapter 6 in this volume) illustrates the importance of
the regional dimension as an important feature of the adjustment
experience in the fishing industry in Atlantic Canada.

The household

One of the distinguishing features of the current macro-economic-policy
climate is that it encourages the marketization of previously non-market
economic activities. Thus non-waged, household-based activities (those
responsible for subsistence agriculture, care and maintenance of children and elders, and so on) are discouraged through changing incentives in the economy. At the same time, household-support services
provided by the state (education, health, food subsidies, transport subsidies, for example) are being withdrawn. This leaves a tremendous
resource gap which creates tensions and 'rigidities' in the adjusting
economy. However, macro-economists have no formal view of the
household as a gendered economic unit, nor of the relation between
market and non-market activities.

A crucial aspect of adjustment, which has not been evaluated in any
systematic way, is the relation between market and non-market activities (see Part I of this volume). This is where incorporating the 'household' into an analysis of macro-economic reform is essential. For
example, in my experience of evaluating the employment effects of
structural adjustment, it was not possible to compare the situation
'before' adjustment with that 'after' it, since certain industries rely on
the shift of labour resources from non-market activities (household-
based) to market-based work in the clothing industry. In order to
examine the full economic and social impact of adjustment and develop a clearer picture, evaluation of macro-economic policies should
combine anthropological and sociological family data sets with economic data on women. For example, given the propensity to employ
young women in certain of the new labour-intensive industries, it is
important to know where responsibility for their household-based tasks
has been distributed, and how their departure affects the division of
labour within the household. In Indonesia, certain firms recruit female
labour from distant villages, and families of girls may be recruited as
a unit. They live and work together, with the older sister taking responsibility for the training and discipline of the younger sisters. In such
cases, growth in female employment is accompanied by a very compli-

cated set of factors within the household as well as within the enterprise. Adjustment tends to create a tension within the household: on the one hand, the marketization of economic activities is encouraged, but on the other, conditions for the 'production and reproduction of human beings' worsen as the costs of public services and foodstuffs rise. Given the central importance of the household as a social and economic structure, it should be included as a unit of analysis within the adjustment framework.

Statistical analysis

How does one begin to evaluate the gender impact of policy reform? Statistical analysis can provide part of the answer when used as part of a broad-based multidisciplinary approach to the evaluation of macro-economic policies. It can provide a broad picture of important relationships among quantifiable phenomena such as wages, employment, female educational attainment rates, mortality rates and certain macro-economic changes – devaluation, rising interest rates, patterns of government spending, general trends in GDP, and so on. However, this type of analysis is of limited value on its own. There are considerable conceptual difficulties in isolating the impact of stabilization and adjustment policies on any given variable. Equally, how does one quantify policy regimes? How can we tell whether failure is due to policy implementation or the lack of it? As a start, there are three commonly applied approaches to statistical analysis which could be relevant to gender-sensitive research[3] (i) the 'before/after' approach, which could be used to compare the relative status of women and men before and after implementation of the macro-economic (and trade) reforms; (ii) the 'with/without' approach, which can provide a means to compare gender differentials in countries that have implemented adjustment programmes with a 'control group' of countries without programmes;[4] (iii) 'pooled regression analysis', using either or both time-series and cross-section data sets.

The evaluation of gender-differentiated effects of macro-economic policy faces the same hurdles as any other impact study. The important variables must be defined and be directly or indirectly quantifiable. Together, the 'before/after' and 'with/without' approaches can provide useful information, despite their weaknesses. For example, the 'before/after' approach attributes all observed changes to the adjustment reforms; the 'with/without' approach assumes that both countries are subject to the same external factors and have similar internal characteristics. Mosley et al. (1991) provide a clear description of the counter-factual and present refinements to the methodology, which compares the performance of a control group with matched pairs of countries in the analysis.

The only type of gender-based information that can be analysed is that which can be quantified. Such information could include direct variables such as female education levels, employment participation rates, wages, and so on. Given the absence of gender-specific data, however, much of the statistical analysis of the differential effects of policies on men and women would have to rely on proxy indicators of women's and men's status. Clearly the choice of proxies requires a detailed understanding of the subject area.

In addition to the counterfactual approach, one can glean useful information from regression analysis. There are three types of regression analysis: (i) time-series; (ii) cross-section; and (iii) time-series and cross-section combined.[5] Time-series analysis can be useful if a country has good data sources covering a minimum of ten years. One can compare changes in certain indicators – for example, the male to female wage differential – over time and then compare the statistical significance of the reforms in explaining the changes in the ratios. In practice, the scarcity of gender-disaggregated data, particularly over long periods of time, means that the time-series approach has limited applications until a stock of gender-disaggregated time-series data is accumulated.

The second approach is useful for comparing snapshots of a society and can be used in the type of counterfactual analysis discussed in Mosely et al. (1991). Survey data which are often gender-disaggregated can be used for this type of analysis. A major problem with 'snapshots' is that they are often not comparable over time. The third technique can be useful for analysing gender-related variables, since data sets which cover a short period of time can be used. For example, survey data available for several regions but for only a limited number of years can yield useful statistical information.

Data availability places a significant constraint on the statistical analysis of the gender effects of macro-economic reform. The most commonly used international data sets have no or very little gender-disaggregated data: International Financial Statistics – none; World Bank – few; Unido – very few; ILO Labour Statistics – patchy; ILO October Enquiry – contains occupation-specific employment data. Country-specific sources – national census, household surveys, village/town-specific surveys, national labour-market surveys, and so on – will often contain relevant detailed information. However, it is often found that the categories change between data sets and over time. These types of data can be used in cross-section analysis and are useful for building up a descriptive picture of the phenomena to be explained. They can also provide information useful for constructing models of the economy.

Model building

In view of the poor quality and limited availability of useful gender-disaggregated data, the judgements that can be made on the basis of the data alone are often very tentative. Therefore detailed case studies, which incorporate the levels of disaggregation discussed earlier in this chapter, provide a better basis for evaluating the social and economic phenomena associated with macro-economic reforms under structural adjustment programmes. However, even with this sort of information available, it is often difficult to visualize the interconnections in an economy. How do rising interest rates, devaluation, cuts in government investment, and so on, affect the relative status of men and women? Simple models can provide a framework for answering this type of question. Many economic models have been constructed using a limited amount of macro-economic information, combined with judgements about central relationships in the economy. Any formalization of the relationship between quantifiable phenomena constitutes a simple model. It is common practice to make very general assumptions about relationships within an economy, and all models suffer to some extent from oversimplistic assumptions. But there is no theoretical or practical justification for the neglect of gender in macro-economic models. For example, in a recent study of changes in the sectoral structure of poverty in Indonesia during a period of macro-economic adjustment, poverty profiles were summarized for a number of economic categories (self-employed, wage labourers, urban, rural), and changes in incidence of poverty were evaluated at a relatively disaggregated level, comparing household-survey data which spanned the adjustment period (Huppi and Ravallion, 1991). There is no reason why this type of analysis cannot be repeated, with a further gender-disaggregation of categories. This information could then be utilized within a simple model of the dynamics of adjustment. Take the rise in the price of tradeables relative to non-tradeables as an example, since this is a central component of the adjustment regime. High prices for tradeables benefit exporters and hurt importers. They may also benefit those indirectly involved in production for export and constitute a disincentive to those who produce for the home market, or who rely on imports. How these policies interact with the relative status of women is quite complicated and will depend on the role of women as producers (paid and unpaid) and as consumers of both tradeable and non-tradeable goods. For example, the change in policy environment may actually improve the position of some women as producers (if they work in export sectors), but their position as consumers or producers in essential non-traded activities (the household) may deteriorate. This type of problem lends itself to gender-sensitive macro-economic modelling, where the implications of various macro-economic policies can be traced through the economy to the meso- and micro-levels. The purpose here is not to discuss in any detail the nature of macro-economic models, but rather to point to areas where improvements can be made in our analytic tools for explaining the dynamics of macro-economic reform, and particularly the gender aspects of reform. Although many models are highly complicated and require specialist knowledge, it is possible to construct a technically simple and workable model without possessing highly specialized quantitative skills. This is a potentially useful tool with which to analyse gender-sensitive interrelationships between macro-economic phenomena and those of a meso or micro nature. Modelling, combined with in-depth qualitative analysis, represents a potential step forward in the analysis of the gender implications of macro-economic reform.

Notes

1. This research was financed by the Leverhulme Trust.
2. For a critical discussion of resource 'switching' during adjustment, see Elson, 1991.
3. This section draws on Kirkpatrick and Evers, 1992.
4. Mosley et al. (1991) present a modification of this methodology so that the comparison of with/without is made between countries with similar characteristics in an effort to compare like with like.
5. For a more rigorous discussion of regression analysis for policy evaluation, see Goldstein and Montiel, 1986.

References

Afshar, Haleh and Carolyne Dennis (eds) (1992) *Women and Adjustment in the Third World*. Macmillan, Basingstoke.

Berry, A. (forthcoming) *Public Support Systems for Small and Medium Exporters*. World Bank, Washington DC.

Elson, Diane (1989) 'The Impact of Structural Adjustment on Women: Concepts and Issues'. In Bade Onimode (ed.) *The IMF, The World Bank and the African Debt*, Vol. 2, The Social and Political Impact. Zed Books, London.

—— (1991) *Male Bias in the Development Process*. Manchester University Press, Manchester.

Evers, B. (1992) 'Trade Liberalisation and Employment in the Indonesian Manufacturing Sector'. Conference Paper, Nottingham University Development Studies Association, September.

Goldstein, M. and P. Montiel (1986) 'Evaluating Fund Stabilization Programs with Multi-country Data: Some Methodological Pitfalls'. In *IMF Staff Papers*, vol. 33, no. 2.

Huppi, M. and M. Ravallion (1991) 'The Sectoral Structure of Poverty During an Adjustment Period: Evidence for Indonesia in the Mid-1980s'. In *World Development*, vol. 19, no. 12.

International Labour Office (1989) 'Labour Market Issues and Structural Adjustment', World Employment Programme Conference Papers. Employment and Development Department, ILO, Geneva.

Kirkpatrick, C. and B. Evers (1992) 'The Impact of Trade Liberalisation On Industrial Sector and Labour Market Performance'. Working paper, Asian Regional Team for Employment Promotion, World Employment Programme, International Labour Organisation, New Delhi.

Manning, C. (1992) 'Survey of Recent Developments'. In *Bulletin of Indonesian Economic Studies*, vol. 28, no. 1.

Mosley, P. (1991) 'Structural Adjustment: A General Overview, 1980–89'. In V.N. Balasubramanyam and S. Lall (eds) *Current Issues in Development Economics*. Macmillan, Basingstoke.

Mosley, P., J. Harrigan and J. Toye (1991) *Aid and Power: The World Bank and Policy-based Lending*. 2 vols. Routledge, London.

Page, S. (1991) *Trade, Finance and Developing Countries, Strategies and Constraints in the 1990s*. Harvester Wheatsheaf for the Overseas Development Institute, Hemel Hempstead.

Standing, G. (1989) 'Global Feminisation through Flexible Labour'. In *World Development*, vol. 17, no. 7.

Thee, Kian Wee (1991) 'The Surge of Asian NIC Investment into Indonesia'. In *Bulletin of Indonesian Economic Studies*, vol. 27, no. 3.

Thorbecke, E. (1992) *Adjustment and Equity in Indonesia*, OECD Development Centre, Paris.

9

Turkish Women and Structural Adjustment
Nilufer Cagatay

This chapter presents an overview of changes in the gender pattern of employment that accompanied the reorientation of the Turkish economy in the 1980s from import-substitution industrialization to export-oriented manufacturing. This reorientation was achieved through a variety of IMF/World Bank-supervised policies covering foreign trade, subsidies, interest rates, currency devaluation, privatization of public enterprises, public-sector reform, and incentives for foreign investment. At the same time, a military coup in September 1980 fundamentally changed the nature of the labour policy established during the import-substitution industrialization (ISI) period, which was one of significant trade-union growth in Turkey. In the early 1980s the government restricted union activities. Thus structural adjustment and macro-economic stabilization policies were accompanied by political repression, although this was eroded in the course of the decade as a result of struggles for democratization.

The reduction in labour standards and the consequent erosion of wages are familiar aspects of structural adjustment policies undertaken during the 1980s in many Third World countries. Another aspect of structural adjustment policies is the move toward more 'flexible' forms of production[1] – the 'informalization' and 'decentralization' of employment whereby companies rely more on part-time, casual or temporary workers, the subcontracting of production and/or use of home-workers. These strategies of labour management reduce employees' income and job security, thereby helping to shift onto workers the costs and risks associated with uncertain and unstable markets. Standing (1989) has argued that, in many economies in the 1980s, these changes in labour practices have been accompanied by the 'feminization of employment' in the sense of an absolute and relative growth in the use of women's labour, partly through the substitution of women for men workers. Standing has referred to these changes in both employment conditions and the gender composition of employment as 'feminization through flexible labour', and has further argued that this phenomenon is global and results from structural adjustment, as well as from an increasing interest in 'flexibility' on the part of employers.[2] At the same time, studies into women's employment position during the course of industrialization indicate the relatively high concentration of women in export-oriented industries, lending support to the argument that export-oriented production leads to the feminization of employment.[3] Two implications of Standing's thesis are that sex segregation per se becomes less significant as employers substitute women for men in the search for cheap labour, and that the wage gap between men and women narrows as women's unemployment rate decreases and men's unemployment increases. Women are less segregated in the economy and begin to enter sectors and occupations which are gender-typed as male. Standing argues that although in the short run this trend represents a 'gain' for women in the 'crude sense', in the long run it is detrimental for both men and women, since everybody's work conditions deteriorate. Standing's thesis is a powerful one, linking micro- and macro-levels of analysis by examining the implications of macro-economic policies for firms' competitive strategies, their gender-specific implications, as well as the behaviour of men and women as potential and actual workers. Nonetheless, Turkish case studies reveal some problematic aspects of the feminization thesis.[4]

According to aggregate data on labour-force statistics, historically women in Turkey have constituted more than 35 per cent of the economically active population, even though their share registered a gradual fall from 43.11 per cent to 36.06 per cent between 1955 and 1980, and a slight fall between 1980 and 1985 to 35.44 per cent. This trend is the result of a structural shift in the economy and the population from rural to urban areas, where women's labour-force participation rates are much lower than in the rural areas. Throughout the 1980s, this trend overrode any possible dynamic toward economy-wide feminization. It remains to be seen whether this trend will change to give rise to the U-shaped pattern of women's labour-force participation observed in economies more industrialized than Turkey's. An understanding of feminization, therefore, has to start with the separation of trends in female employment from the effects of particular macro/industrialization policies.

The degree of overall segregation in the Turkish economy can be assessed by the dissimilarity index (DI) calculated by Cagatay and Berik (1990). The dissimilarity indices calculated on the basis of the Standard Industrial Classification (SIC) one-digit level census data register a slight decrease between 1970 and 1975 from 35.4 to 32.85. However, the index increases sharply between 1975 and 1980 to 43.28 while it remains at a stable level of 43.25 in 1985. In comparison to nine other countries (all of which are industrialized economies) for which dissimilarity indices are available, the degree of measured gender segregation in Turkey was the highest in 1980 and 1985 while it was the median figure in 1975.[5] Thus, at the level of the economy as a whole, there is no evidence of 'feminization' of labour in the sense of an increase in the female share of employment. Neither was there a decrease in the overall degree of gender segregation in the 1980s.

In spite of the considerable industrialization that has taken place in Turkey, an overwhelming proportion of women continue to work in agriculture. According to the 1985 census, 86.5 per cent of all women participating in the labour force were in the agricultural sector, while the comparable figure for men was 43 per cent. On the other hand, women have constituted about half the labour force in agriculture since the 1950s. However, the 1985 census figures indicate that women constituted only 11.95 per cent of the labour force in non-agricultural sectors.

Another way of looking at this phenomenon is by analysing the urban labour force separately. Women's low economic-activity rate in the urban areas is, indeed, in sharp contrast to rural areas. During the 1980s, women in rural areas made up 41–42 per cent of the labour force, while in urban areas they accounted for between 14 per cent in 1982 and 18.83 per cent in 1989. This increase is attributable to women's increasing labour-force participation in the 1980s, from 11.2 per cent in 1982 to a high point of 17.2 per cent in 1989, while in 1990 there was a decrease to 15.2 per cent. Thus there was a process of feminization in the urban areas in the 1980s.

Another striking feature of the urban labour markets, however, is the very high unemployment rates faced by women in the urban sector compared to the low unemployment rates for rural women. During the 1980s, the former experienced unemployment rates ranging from 23 per cent in 1982 to 33.2 per cent in 1985, while for urban men the comparable figures in the corresponding years were 9 per cent and 11.6 per cent. Unemployment rates for urban women and men in 1989 and 1990 indicate a stabilization around 26.5 per cent and 10.7 per cent respectively. Even though women's share of the urban labour force was 18.83 per cent at its highest level in 1989, women constituted more than one-third of the urban unemployed except in 1982 and 1983. Therefore unemployment in Turkey is, first and foremost, an urban female phenomenon. Moreover, this situation is particularly acute for young women aged between 15 and 24 years, whose unemployment rate in 1990 was 40 per cent, while the figure for men of the same age group was 21 per cent. The highest unemployment rate (26.9 per cent) for urban boys is in the 12–14 age group (SIS, 1991: 126–7). Urban women also tend to be unemployed for a longer period than men. Again, according to 1990 figures, 51.6 per cent of the urban unemployed women were without a job for more than one year, while the comparable figure for men is 42.3 per cent (SIS, 1991: 131). Furthermore, the higher unemployment rates women face also seem to affect their participation rates in the urban economy. Throughout the 1980s, women constituted about two-thirds of those urban workers who have given up looking for work. That means twice as many women as men have dropped out of the urban labour force. The increase in urban women's labour-force participation rates supports Standing's feminization thesis. But this increased participation contributed more to feminization of unemployment than to the feminization of employment: while Standing predicted a fall in female unemployment rates and a rise in male unemployment rates, in the Turkish urban economy the opposite occurred.

Women's higher unemployment rates and longer periods of unemployment are not primarily caused by their lower educational achievement in general. While women's participation in the labour force is a function of their level of education (the higher the level of education, the higher is the participation rate), women of all educational categories suffered from higher unemployment rates than did men with the same level of education, with the exception of graduates of vocational junior high schools whose male and female unemployment rates were the same in 1990 (SIS, 1991: 94). Women with high-school certificates experience the highest unemployment rate, of 35 per cent, while for women university graduates the figure is 12.8 per cent, compared to 14 per cent and 5.8 per cent respectively for men. These figures point to the greater difficulties faced by women in the labour markets when compared to men with the same formal educational qualifications. They clearly do not suggest a decline in the significance of gender segregation per se, as argued by Standing.

There were also changes in women's income and earnings position in the urban economy during the 1980s. Even though detailed wage series are not available for a precise assessment of women's relative wage position, some 'crude' estimates indicate a deterioration in women's incomes vis-à-vis men's. During 1978–79, on average, a wage/salary-earning woman received a disposable income equal to 69.9 per cent of that of a wage/salary-earning man; in 1987, this figure fell to 67.99 per cent.[6]

Focusing on manufacturing as a likely site for 'feminization', Cagatay and Berik (1990, 1994) found no evidence of feminization of the manufacturing labour force, as recorded in census or annual manufacturing survey data. One type of activity which seems to be growing and contributing to feminization of manufacturing in the 1980s, however, is home-working, which is dominated by women. The Household Labour

Force Surveys (HLFS), conducted six-monthly since 1988, provide better insights into this activity, which is an indicator of both flexibility and feminization. Since no comparable data on home-working for the late 1970s or 1980s exists, it is hard to assess its growth. However, two recent studies on women home-workers in urban Turkey suggest that this activity has grown as a result of export-led industrialization (ELI) (Lordoglu, 1990; and Cinar, 1991) since some (although not all) home-working activities involve clothes production for external markets. Cinar observes that home-working provides employers with low wage costs, low overhead costs and flexible production to cope with fluctuations in market demand. Indeed, the HLFS data also reveal a more volatile female urban manufacturing employment compared to male employment. Furthermore, the volatility in women's employment is greater in home-working manufacturing as opposed to formal factory manufacturing. This is, indeed, an indication of flexibility and to some extent an indication of feminization of one component of the urban economy, given that home-workers constituted between 18 and 25.67 per cent of all urban women manufacturing workers between 1988 and 1990. There is also reason to believe that the HLFS underestimate the numbers of home-workers. Cinar estimates 88,000 for 1988 and 1989 in Istanbul alone; the figures recorded in the surveys for all urban areas are 82,802 and 65,911 during October 1988 and April 1989 respectively. The extent of home-working, and therefore of female employment, is higher than that revealed in the surveys. One reason for this underrecording is that some women carry out this activity secretly without telling their husbands. For married women home-workers who tend to have received little or no education, home-working provides the only available option, especially as about half the husbands do not allow wives to work outside the home. Thus, the 'alliance' of patriarchal relations that shape the lives of this particular group of women and the particular industrialization strategy of the 1980s have created a small female employment niche.

It is important to keep in mind, however, that this phenomenon does not point to either economy-wide or urban feminization; it is limited in scope. Neither does it represent a decreasing significance of gender segregation per se. On the contrary, it is the result of gender segregation prevailing among a particular class. To the extent that the activities involved, such as knitting, embroidery, ready-made clothes production, are typically female-dominated activities in the formal manufacturing sector, they do not represent a feminization of the type conceptualized by Standing via substitution of women for men. Rather, they represent a change in the form of organization of production of activities that are generally dominated by women (see Elson, 1991).

Notes

1. During the 1980s, moves toward more flexible forms of production were observed in advanced capitalist countries as well (see Cohen, Chapter 7 in this volume). For a discussion of labour standards in the global economy see Herzenberg and Perez-Lopes, 1990.

2. See Standing, 1989 for an elaboration of the concept and empirical evidence for Third World economies as well as industrialized countries; Elson, 1991 for a critique and clarification of the conceptual issues; and Berik and Cagatay, 1992b for a methodological and empirical critique of Standing's feminization thesis.

3. See Berik and Cagatay, 1992, for econometric evidence that the share of exports in an industry's output is significant in explaining the share of female employment in that industry and in controlling a number of other factors for Turkey both during the ISI period and during the period of export-oriented manufacturing.

4. A similar investigation was undertaken for women in Turkish manufacturing in Cagatay and Berik, 1990 and 1994, and for urban women in Cagatay, 1991.

5. The value of DI ranges from 0 to 100, with 0 corresponding to no sex segregation and 100 indicating complete sex segregation. For further discussion, see Cagatay and Berik, 1990.

6. These figures are based on data from 1978–79 Urban Places Household Income and Consumption Expenditures Survey Results (SIS, 1982: 64) and 1987 Household Income and Consumption Expenditures Survey Results (SIS, 1990: 468). The figures need to be regarded with some caution since the definition of 'urban' in the 1978–79 survey was 'settlements with a population of 10,000 or more', while in the 1987 survey the definition was 'settlements with a population of 20,000 or more'. However, this change of definition would tend to bias the 1987 figures so as to bring wage-earning women's incomes closer to those of wage-earning men. These figures are not a measure of wage differences as such, since they refer to the average income received from all sources (including rent, interest, etc.) by wage earners. Nonetheless, they would largely reflect average wage differences between women and men. For 1978–79, the ratio of average urban female to male wages was 72.7 per cent. It is not possible to calculate the same ratio for 1987 from published data.

References

Agarwal, B., B. Bergmann, M. Floro and N. Folbre (eds) (1992) *Women and Work in the World Economy*. New York University Press, New York.

Berik, Gunseli and Nilufer Cagatay (1992) 'Industrialization Strategies and Gender Composition of Manufacturing Employment in Turkey'. In G. Berik and N. Cagatay, 'How Global is "Global Feminisation" through Flexible Labour?'. Unpublished ms.

Cagatay, Nilufer (1991) 'Turkish Women in the Urban Economy'. Paper presented at MESA Meeting, Washington DC, November.

Cagatay, Nilufer and Gunseli Berik (1990) 'Transition to Export-led Growth in Turkey: Is There a Feminization of Employment?' In *Review of Radical Political Economics*, vol. 22, no. 1.

────── (1994) 'What has Export-oriented Manufacturing Meant for Turkish Women Workers?' In Pam Sparr (ed.) *Structural Adjustment and Women in the Third World.* Zed Books, London.

Cinar, E. Mine (1991) *Labor Market Opportunities for Adult Female and Home-working Women in Istanbul, Turkey.* Working Paper No. 2, The G.E. von Grunebaum Center for Near East Studies, University of California, Los Angeles.

Elson, D. (1991) 'Appraising Recent Developments in the World Market for Nimble Fingers: Accumulation, Regulation, Organization'. ISS, The Hague.

Herzenberg, Stephen and Jorge F. Perez-Lopes (eds) (1990) *Labor Standards and Development in the Global Economy.* US Department of Labor, Washington DC.

Lordoglu, Kuvvet (1990) *Eve Is Verme Sistemi Icinde Kadin Isqucu Uzerine Bir Alan Arastirmasi.* Friedrich Ebert Vakfi, Istanbul.

Standing, Guy (1989) 'Global Feminisation Through Flexible Labor'. In *World Development*, vol. 17, no. 7.

State Institute of Statistics (SIS) (1982) *Urban Places Household Income and Consumption Expenditures Survey Results*, No. 999. Ankara.

────── (1990a) *1988 Household Labor Force Survey Results*, No. 1433. Ankara.

────── (1990b) *1987 Income Distribution: Household Income and Expenditure Survey Results*, No. 1441. Ankara.

────── (1991a) *1989 April Household Labor Force Survey Results*, No. 1445. Ankara.

────── (1991b) *1989 October Household Labor Force Survey Results*, No. 1453. Ankara.

────── (1991c) *1990 April Household Labor Force Survey Results*, No. 1455. Ankara.

Mexican Rural Women Wage Earners and Macro-economic Policies
Antonieta Barrón

Some considerations on the global economy

A recent phenomenon in capitalism's development is the so-called globalization of the economy, which is basically the decentralization and internationalization of productive processes. This internationalization, a continuation of the expansionary forms of capital which intensified in the 1970s, has led to a differential development of technology among countries and a new international division of labour. Several factors have contributed to this globalization phenomenon, including technological innovation in transport and communications, which has allowed time and cost reductions in the exchange of products and information; large wage differences between industrialized and developing countries; and differences in the intensity of labour and the growing international competition for markets, which necessitate a reduction in production costs, resulting in an increase in international levels of competition (Quintanilla, 1991).

Globalization in the Mexican context is more evident in the manufacturing sector and in oil where capital, technology, the market and labour processes are all integrated. In agriculture, it takes different forms due to the specific national characteristics of this sector, and has occurred in the context of the internationalization of production processes. Production factors, inputs and labour come either from other countries (mainly the United States) or from local sources. As regards capital, it may originate from various foreign sources.[1]

The transnationalization of Mexican agriculture intensified in the 1970s, coinciding with changes in the crops cultivated and the country's loss of self-sufficiency in food. This process, which has taken place mainly among fruit and vegetable export producers, who, under the Free Trade Agreement (FTA), are expected to cultivate 150,000 hectares

(Calava, 1991) with tropical fruits and vegetables, will lead to further technological dependence combined with a greater reliance on foreign capital. The seeds for the crops are mainly produced in the United States and imported by the Mexican growers;[2] an accompanying technology determines the work processes and consequently the number and intensity of the labour force employed: large contingents of workers are hired from the time the seed is sown until the fruit is picked. It follows that changes have occurred in the labour markets involved in this dynamic of internationalization. The evolution of labour in agriculture depends not only on those factors related to supply, but also on expansion of the cultivated area and the technology used.

In most analyses of the expansion of export crops, the fundamental component, the labour force, is omitted. This chapter will concentrate on the way the labour market is formed in relation to vegetable production. In the agricultural sector an expansion in the cultivation of labour-intensive export crops – fruit and vegetables – enabled women to become wage earners. It was estimated that in 1990, nationwide, approximately 20 per cent of all wage earners were women; however, this figure varies according to sector and activity. In agriculture female labour represents, on average, approximately 15 per cent of the total, but in the area of fruit and vegetables about 50 per cent female labour is involved. The feminization of the labour markets in fruit and vegetable cultivation was accompanied by a marked deterioration in women's living and working conditions. Reductions in public spending, changes in laws governing land property rights, and changes in credit facilities were contributing factors to this deterioration.

This study, then, focuses on rural women wage earners, and takes as its point of reference those occupied in vegetable production, the most important female labour market in Mexico. To this end I use information obtained in a survey conducted between 1988 and 1990 in the districts of Tlayuacapan, Atlatlahucan and Yecapixtla in the state of Morelos; in Actopan and Ixmiquilpan in the state of Hidalgo; in Autlan in the state of Jalisco; in Villa de Arista in the state of San Luis Potosi; in Huatabampo, Sonora and in San Quintin, Baja California.[3] The thesis is advanced that there are limits to the feminization of the labour force in this sector, connected to changing technologies, labour-supply factors and land-reform measures. The rise in female activity in this area, which is characterized by extensive migration between the various agricultural producers throughout the year, is part of a larger process signalling families' inability to reproduce themselves. We find that constant migration, in conjunction with poor health and inadequate provision of public-sector support (such as day care for workers' children), has led to an increase in women's daily workload.

Table 10.1 Working days needed per hectare for different crops

Crop	Days
Corn	38
Beans	35
Rice	37
Wheat	12
Soya	35
Sorghum	31
Cartamo	18
Ground tomato*	66
Tomato	692
Cucumber	192
Melon	150

* A tomato vine that grows on the ground without any support.

Source: SARH and UNPH, selected years.

The production process for vegetables

In the cultivation of vegetable and fruit crops for export, an expansion in both the area cultivated and the geographic mobility of the crops was observed. Various factors contributed to this expanded production. The most important was an increase in demand in the US. For example, total exports of tomatoes to the US in 1970 amounted to 158,200 tons; by 1989 this figure had reached 415,600 tons. Other vegetables, such as green chillies,[4] peas, asparagus, cabbage, onions, and so on, grew from 169,500 to 700,000 in the same period. This increase was due to the lowering of US government restrictions on these products, general increase in demand, and the reduction of cultivated land in California and Florida. Another favourable factor was a liberalization in policy governing individual and joint capital investment with Mexican producers. The main factor attracting investors was the low cost of labour. Thus the cultivated area for fruit and vegetables for export expanded from 276,800 hectares in 1970 to 500,000 in 1985, rising to 700,000 hectares by 1980, representing 3.5 per cent of the total land cultivated. Although this percentage is relatively small, the absorption of labour is much higher than for other crops due to the large numbers of workers required per hectare (see Table 10.1). It is estimated that fruit and vegetable production absorbs almost 25 per cent of the economically active rural population, of which 50 per cent are women and 15 per cent are children under the age of fourteen.

The vegetable and fruit labour market

These labour markets are not homogeneous; they can be divided into secondary (less developed) and primary (more developed) sectors. Secondary markets provide products for the national market and are dominated by small and 'mini' landowners. Their dependence on the international market is basically through the purchase of seeds. Primary markets are characterized by the large capitalist producers, who coexist with the small and medium producers. A close relationship is maintained between these latter markets and the producers from Sinaloa, the stronger of whom having packing plants in San Quintin, Baja California; Villa de Arista, San Luis Potosi; and Autlan, Jalisco. (Often the seedlings and small plants for tomatoes, sown by the capitalist producers in other parts of the country, also come from Sinaloa.) These markets produce for export, with the rejected produce sold on the national market. Differences between primary and secondary markets also find expression in the division of labour operating within them. Primary markets have a rigid division of labour; in secondary markets this is only just beginning to take place.[5]

Characteristics of labour

Since the 1970s it has been argued that the incorporation of women into wage labour occurs in unstable markets with low productivity and low wages. In the case of vegetable production, however, this is no longer true. Here we are dealing with labour markets that provide work for ten months of the year, as crops are cultivated during the cycles of spring to summer and autumn to winter; the unstable seasonal nature of the activity has thus been greatly reduced.[6] Women, then, have begun to participate in high-productivity labour markets that pay better wages and guarantee employment for the best part of a year. However, the forms of hiring and the 'contracts' given, along with inadequate living and working conditions, are the factors that present problems. On these issues, the state has not committed itself to regulation. Furthermore, in the secondary markets, with their small volume of production and limited economic capacity, only local labour is employed; labourers are never contracted from elsewhere. In primary markets, both the local population, and transported and migrant labour are hired.

The characteristics of labour supply in relation to sex and age depend on the nature of the work and the technology used. In examining the primary markets, it is evident that men, women and children, mostly Indian and with little schooling, are hired for vegetable picking. In this group the majority are illiterate, although an increase in educational level has been observed – some workers having attended both primary and secondary school. Variations in the numbers of children employed are due to the absolute shortage of adults. (In our case studies we found that 15 per cent of the workers were children under fourteen.) Children's labour thus acts as an adjustable input in this production process.

One of the most striking features of this labour market is the way women have increased their participation. In our sample of 1,971 workers, 53 per cent were women, of whom 48.3 per cent were nineteen years of age or less and 51 per cent over twenty; of these, 70 per cent were married. Given the present course of expansion in vegetable production, and the fact that in the near future the statutory size of the cultivated areas is to be extended, it is likely that producers will have sustained recourse to the female labour force. The feminization of this labour market, however, may be limited by the supply of labour, the way the fruit is collected (the technology used), and the modifications made to Article 27 of the Mexican Constitution, which allows for communal (*ejidal*)[7] lands to be sold or to be cultivated in conjunction with private capital, as well as ending the practice of land sharing.

Several elements of this hypothesis warrant discussion. The opening up of regions dedicated to fruit and vegetable production is likely to lead to a fall in world prices due to supply exceeding demand. Parallel to this, the liberalization of labour, '*los ejidatarios*', will put pressure on labour supply, resulting in a wage fall unless the vegetable and fruit markets expand and/or other crops are cultivated to compete in other markets, such as in the Pacific Rim countries. In fresh fruit and vegetable packing, as well as in the frozen and pre-cooked processes – work which is carried out elsewhere, a female labour force will predominate. When the packing is done on the production site, men will be added to the workforce, unless the women can keep up with the pace of this work or there is a shortage of male labour. In all primary markets, packing and production labour is short in the picking seasons, which last for two months. This relative shortage and the flexibility within labour markets has led to competition among producers and, fortunately, to wage rises in other regions and sectors, as we shall see later.

Finally, changes in the Constitution will result in a recomposition of the labour force in the labour-intensive export crop sector, because the liberalization of the very small landholdings will increase the labour supply, especially men's labour. There will also be an increase in flows of migrant peasants, forced off their land, towards the border regions where an expansion of agricultural activity is expected. This will modify the sex and age composition of the labour markets. It is, however, difficult to imagine that this 'liberated' labour force will migrate to the cities; they are more likely to get work in the country, and wages are higher in the border areas.

Migration patterns

Although the main motive for migration is a family's inability to reproduce itself in its place of origin, its destination – that is, the place it migrates to – also plays a role in offering better employment and wages. Whether the migration is from agricultural or non-agricultural areas, it is generated by access to employment in the labour markets. In this respect migration from the country to the city presents greater uncertainty today than inter-rural migration. Furthermore, rural-to-urban migration is usually individual, while rural-to-rural migration allows the whole family to move.

In the regions studied[8] the exodus of the population takes place at an early age: 30.4 per cent of the men and 50 per cent of the women are nineteen years old or less (see Table 10.2). The temporary-permanent immigrants,[9] although predominantly young people, are a heterogeneous group: lone adults, or families with children who leave school to migrate with their parents, and young girls who helped with the housework or worked the family's plot of land. The research confirms what was known at the beginning of the 1980s: there is a predominance of female migration over male, with sexual differences also marked by age. Some 68 per cent of the males migrate between the ages of 15 and 29, the dominant group being between 20 and 24, the optimum working age. On the other hand, even though the majority of women are 24 years old or under (66.7 per cent), those between 15 and 19 predominate. It might be expected that the proportion of women between 25 and 29 would be substantially lower; the fact that this is not the case indicates that motherhood is no longer an obstacle to entering the labour market. While men's participation decreases with age, women's rates increase slightly between the ages of 45 and 49 – the classic case of women who have completed their reproductive cycle, along with others who find no barriers to being employed.

A tendency exists towards specialization in the agricultural activity of vegetable and fruit production. None of those interviewed in all occupations had migrated to find work harvesting crops other than vegetables. Workers from Guerrero and Oaxaca migrate from their village to Villa de Arista, San Luis Potosi; and from there to Autlan, Jalisco; and finally to Viliacan, Sinaloa. Some from Sinaloa pass over to Baja California. The selectors and packers mainly leave Sinaloa for other areas. Some travel further, from Morelos to Sinaloa, from there to San Quintin to Villa Arista; this allows them to be hired most of the year

Table 10.2 Structure of migrant population by age in Autlan, Jalisco; Villa de Arista, San Luis Potosi; and San Quintin, Baja California

Age	Men	%	Women	%
up to 14	20	7.8	44	13.6
15–19	58	22.6	118	36.4
20–24	75	29.2	54	16.7
25–29	41	16.0	30	9.3
30–34	20	7.8	26	8.0
35–39	19	7.4	23	7.1
40–44	11	4.3	9	2.8
45–49	4	1.6	11	3.4
50–54*	8	3.1	8	2.5
60+	1	0.2	1	0.2
Total	257	100.0	324	100.0

* No population was found between 55 and 59 years old.

Source: Author's research, 1988, 1989 and 1990.

round. These migrations take place among vast areas of capitalist agricultural production with strong links between them. The large Sinaloan producers have fields and packing plants in all regions with the exception of Morelos. This allows them to supply the international market all year round and to mobilize the workforce according to their needs.

For example, 36 per cent of the women packers who go to Autlan, Jalisco come from Villa de Arista, San Luis Potosi. After working in Autlan they go on to Sinaloa and then return to Villa Arista. Thus the migratory movements take place as a function of the vegetable crops (mainly the tomato); they are workers who specialize in the picking, selecting and packing of vegetables for export. Circular migrations take place among the Indian workers from their village to the labour market; some widen their route if they have been signed on; others, who know the market better, go on their own, forming currents of migrants following the crops. The exceptions are those migrants planning to pass over the border: they usually go straight to the northern border zones.

Even though other markets have not been studied, it is well known that labour specializes in those crops which are labour-intensive. The orange pickers pick only oranges, the grape pickers only grapes, and so on. In this way wages are guaranteed. Pay by the day is combined with piecework; selectors are paid by the hour, and packers and box assemblers by piece. Piecework increases productivity and makes the workforce more efficient. This accounts for specialization in the tomato crop.[10]

Wages

The specialization of labour, the low supply relative to demand, the seasonal nature of work in any one region, and the forms of payment – all are causing substantial changes to wage rates for workers in the vegetable labour market. From the signing of the first solidarity pact (the Pact for Stability and Economic Growth – PECE) in December 1987, inflation was reduced, but the resultant inertia was not totally eliminated. The annual inflation rate dropped from 159 per cent in 1987 to 51 per cent in 1988; it fell further to 19.2 per cent in 1989, rising to 29.91 per cent in 1990 and dropping again to 13.3 per cent by August 1991. During the years 1988–91 the minimum wage increased at an annual rate of 19.6 per cent. Meanwhile, according to the Banco de México, consumer prices have risen 40 per cent annually, which means a loss of purchasing power in the order of 38 per cent in the three-year period.

As a result of inflationary inertia and wage policies written into the PECE, real wages fell in the period 1987–91. Taking 1987, when the first pact was signed, as the base peso rate, wages fell by 42 per cent from $77.04 in 1987 to $43.99 in October 1991. However, the wage freeze agreed to in the Pact did not prevent growth in the average wage, which began to increase in real terms from 1988 in manufacturing as well as in capital-intensive agriculture. In the 1980s, the proportion of income accruing to wage earners in the gross national product fell in the manufacturing sector from 14.06 per cent in 1980 to 8.7 per cent in 1988, and in agriculture from 19.18 per cent to 13.28 per cent, reflecting a reduction in labour costs. In spite of the fact that total incomes decreased, average wages show a different pattern. Between 1986 and 1989, the average industrial wage fluctuated at a level between 2.17 and 2.53 times the general minimum wage (GMW), whereas in the agricultural sector, until 1988, average wages represented around 14 per cent of the GMW.

Day labourers' wages

Historically, wages in the countryside have been below the legal minimum, an alarming situation if one considers that most agricultural labourers work only temporarily – between 60 and 120 days per year. For vegetable labourers this situation is beginning to change. In our research the day labourers' wage was found not to comply with the traditional wage pattern; even though the sample was taken at different times and in different regions, a tendency towards uniform wage rates was observed in heterogeneous labour markets.

Table 10.3 Evolution of minimum wages by economic zones and average wage in pesos paid to day labourers in the zones studied (1988–91)

State	Period	Minimum wage of day labourer	Average wage	%
Hidalgo	March 1988	6,670.00	3,000.00	45.0
Hidalgo	July–Sept. 1988	6,670.00	3,500.00	52.5
Morelos	Oct.–Nov. 1988	6,670.00	8,125.00	122.0
Jalisco	Dec. 1988	6,670.00	9,000.00	134.9
San Luis Potosi	July 1989	7,640.00	10,000.00	130.9
Sonora	Dec. 1989	8,475.00	12,000.00	141.6
Baja California	June 1990	10,080.00	13,250.00	129.0
Hidalgo	July 1990	8,405.00	12,500.00	148.7
Baja California	July 1991	11,900.00	22,000.00	184.9
Morelos	Oct. 1991	9,920.00	22,000.00	221.8

Note: In 1989, US$1.00 = Mexican $2,680.00; in 1992 US$1.00 = Mexican $3,100.00

Source: National Commission for Minimum Wages and author's own survey carried out on the dates shown.

In Hidalgo, small landholders predominate; in Morelos, the very small; and in Jalisco, Sonora, Baja California and San Luis Potosi, the small producer coexists with capitalist agriculturists. Furthermore, in the first two, production is for the domestic market, and in the latter four for export. Hidalgo, one of the most backward vegetable-growing regions, reported the lowest wage for 1988. At the end of this same year wages in Morelos were significantly higher. Higher wages in Jalisco, San Luis Potosi and Sonora, if considered out of context, could be explained by their relatively high level of development. However, if we compare wages in completely different regions in terms of their products and volumes of production, such as San Quintin, Baja California and Actopan, and Ixmiquilpa, we find that wages in Hidalgo are not only higher than the legal minimum but at a similar rate to those paid in Baja California.

Additional evidence for the hypothesis that a tendency exists towards uniform wages is that for 1991 in two very different regions, Morelos and Baja California, the average wage was the same. At present this represents 1.85 times the legal minimum in the former and 2.22 times in the latter. In these states wages are determined differently; in San Quintin, fringe benefits are included; in Morelos, the labourers refuse to accept less (see Table 10.3). Even though these wages indicate regional averages, the coincidence[11] between such different regions at different times suggests a relationship between the labour markets in vegetable production – whatever the region there is a tendency towards a uniform wage rate.

Wage increases for day labourers are due to several factors: the seasonal needs of producers in each region, which oblige them to contract labourers at whatever cost; the seasonal coincidence among some regions at picking time, which leads to a competition for labour; high productive levels in crops such as red tomatoes, which allow the producer to pay higher wages at picking time to guarantee his labour force; and the expansion of the area of the country cultivated with vegetable crops has led to an increased demand for labour. Another contributory factor is the growing relationship between these labour markets and the occupied labour force, according to our survey results. The majority of the workers specialize and participate only in the labour market for vegetables. Given the link between the distinct regions as regards labour mobility, it is possible that strong competition has developed between vegetable producers in order to obtain labour. Wage increases also contribute to competition among local producers of the same region, between distinct regions, and even between economic sectors. The small producer is forced to pay higher wages, and from one region to another 'fringe benefits' increase. For example, the producers in Autlan, Jalisco give a food hamper at Christmas in order to compete with the contractors in Sinaloa. There is also competition between sectors, especially on the northern border. During the picking season the packing plants compete with the *maquillas* (free-trade zones) to obtain female labour. The former can offer up to twenty times the minimum wage, while the *maquillas* pay 3.5 times the minimum. In not one case did we find pay differences within an occupation based on the sex of the worker. Wage differences do, at times, exist for children, but not for women; even in the most backward regions, their wage is equal to that of men. The wage rises do not serve to eliminate the greater exploitation of agricultural workers relative to industry, however; for not only is piecework combined with daily contracts, but in no case are labourers paid the amounts and given the benefits laid down by Mexican federal labour law. Notwithstanding these wage increases, the cost of labour is still well below the international average, especially in relation to the United States, thereby giving the Mexican producer a comparative advantage.

The Mexican government's insistence on keeping wages down has not been a success. Workers in industry and agriculture have not been prepared to accept low payment: they either demand higher rates or they opt out in favour of some other economic activity. Thus the average wage for day labourers in vegetable growing rose from less than 20 per cent of the legal minimum wage to twice its value between 1988 and 1991. This trend seems to indicate not only an increase and a homologous tendency among the different vegetable-growing regions, but also points to a closing of the gap between remuneration for agricultural labour and the average industrial wage. From another perspective, wage increases, especially among day labourers (for whom the legal minimum in fact long served as a ceiling for rural wages), only reflect the inapplicability of the legal minimum and of the agreements reached in the Pact, at least with regard to wages. On the other hand, this wage increase is a little misleading at present, given that trade unions have all but lost their bargaining capacity (Zapata, 1991).

Living and working conditions

The majority of workers engaged in fruit and vegetable cultivation are 'temporary-permanent': temporary because they work regionally for one season with one employer, and permanent because they work almost all year round. The nature and conditions of their employment constitute them as part of the contingent labour force. The temporary nature of their work means that they are hired without any of the benefits stipulated by labour law. They are not paid for the seventh day of the week or for holidays, nor are they covered by the national health scheme, nor is seniority recognized; what is more, these workers receive no old-age pensions.

Health coverage is only for the period they are working, and frequently the employer exploits a loophole to avoid providing this benefit. For example, a hectare of red tomatoes needs 692 working days with approximately 34 workers, but the owner obtains only ten passes for the local health clinic in case of accident or sickness, and frequently, at the end of the picking season, these are returned. In the case of nonspecialized secondary markets in vegetable and fruit production, made up of small landholders with little capital, even the minimum health benefits are withheld, with producers arguing that they lack the means to take on this extra expense. Accidents at work are frequent, and no indemnity is available to the family of a worker who happens to die as a result, although this is a legal requirement. Frequently, chemical fertilizers are applied by hand and the workers in the field are sprayed along with the crops. In the case of women in the packing plants, the long hours spent standing result in varicose veins; the dust from peas and green chillies causes respiratory problems; and the wax applied to the fruit causes skin diseases. In these latter cases employers provide no chairs, masks or gloves.

Living conditions are even more primitive. It is estimated that 47 per cent of the total female workforce are not single, and of these at least 84 per cent have a child; almost 50 per cent are migrants. When workers are hired locally, they usually have some form of family support; but migrant women migrate with their entire family, which means they face a double burden of waged work and domestic duties, often leading to an eighteen-hour working day. It is in this context that the state's neo-liberal policies, particularly in relation to health, have contributed to the deterioration of living standards among these women workers. The only state-sponsored programme is Mujeres en Solidaridad. This depends on Pronasol (the national solidarity programme), which assists women based in communities but does not readily include rural migrant workers. Pronasol's greatest limitations are that it is a programme with an uncertain budget and that its scope is limited. To engage in an activity, the whole community must participate; in the case of workers, the employer has to make a financial contribution, along with the workers, and Pronasol has to give its approval.

A National Program for Agricultural Day Laborers does exist and concerns itself with problems relating to housing, water and food supplies. However, these are isolated actions which end when the population migrates. In the case of women labourers, the need for day care for their children, including access to educational facilities and cafeterias, has never been seen as a real issue. Given likely cuts in state spending, it is unlikely that these problems will be dealt with.

In Mexico at present a new retirement scheme is being implemented (*sistema de ahorro para el retiro* – SAR); however, the incorporation of temporary rural labourers is not on the national policy agenda. It would in fact be easy for the state to intervene here, but this would mean greater state control over producers' income, an intervention that would undoubtedly meet with stiff opposition.

Final considerations

The fruit and vegetable production sector in Mexico provides an example of the growing feminization of labour. Women's increased involvement in rural agricultural labour, however, has been paradoxical: they have achieved greater access to monetary compensation with average wages higher than the legal minimum, yet their work conditions are poor and reflect back on their own and their family's ability to reproduce themselves. The internationalization of agricultural production has created greater demand for female labour inputs; yet, at the same time, the government's emphasis on neo-liberal economic and social policies leaves women and their families without the necessary infrastructural support, such as health and day care. In addition, the migratory nature of this work means that entire families move from region to region in search of work. In one sense, families remain united (compared to the pattern of rural–urban migration, which, because it involves mainly individuals, tends to separate families), although conditions are difficult and often stretch the resources of all family members. Children, for example, act as a safety valve for adult labour shortages in the production process, thereby forgoing an education. Female children often contribute to maintenance and reproduction and tend the family's plot of land.

To what extent feminization will continue is uncertain. Liberalization policies and the extension of land area cultivated, to reach 150,000 hectares, as well as changes to Article 27 of the Constitution, will create an even greater demand for labour. However, the supply of adult males will also expand, which in the short term will modify the age and composition of the labour force, probably reducing the numbers of children working. Recent wage patterns and the high demand for labour at picking time suggest that there will be further pressure to increase wages.

Economic liberalization laws have been introduced to allow for the penetration of private capital into the countryside in the name of 'modernization'. One of these laws was the modification to Article 27 of the Constitution; the second policy was to grant selective credit to agriculturalists. Small subsistence farmers were declared to be unsuitable to receive bank loans; they must apply instead to Pronasol for credit, which if not repaid within a year, will mean that they are unable to obtain further credit. Government institutions and banks thus give credit only to 'efficient farmers', which in this country are few, given resource limitations. In the short term we can therefore expect both an increase in the rural labour supply and its sexual recomposition, in a labour market in which demand will probably increase. Confronted with these circumstances, the state must intervene to protect workers, and to regulate the forms of payment and the benefits established by Mexican labour law, such as it is.

Notes

1. These aspects have not been studied, but it is safe to assume that such changes are taking place right across the Mexican countryside on the basis of the burgeoning alliance between US capital and Mexican vegetable growers. The country-wide growth of such joint ventures leads us to assume that they are extending their control over national distribution and exports.

2. Both small and large farmers use imported seeds; however, I am unaware whether or not a monopoly exists in relation to seed production.

3. The survey interviewed a total of 1,971 workers occupied in different

capacities within the vegetable-growing business.

4. An increase due in large part to increased demand from Mexicans and North Americans of Mexican descent living in the US.

5. In the secondary markets there are three main occupations: picker, selector and packer. In the primary market, there are additional jobs such as foreman, water fetcher, team leader, time keeper, and so on. In the packing plants a variety of jobs are to be found, including selector, packer, box assembler, box sealer, ticket writer, band supervisor, crane driver, chlorine supervisor, and so on.

6. Furthermore the shortage of labour that producers face during the picking seasons has led them to contract labour by the day. Rural workers have now become highly specialized and migrate within Mexico, following the crops, with some continuing to the border with the intention of crossing into the US. This specialization has led to an increase in wages to around twice the legal minimum, which in Mexico is not bad pay. Vegetable/fruit production in Mexico is highly profitable and has high productivity levels.

7. Lands given by the state to the peasants in usufruct; not to be bought or sold, only inherited.

8. Migration data in the survey relate to Autlan in Jalisco state, and Villa Arista in San Luis Potosi.

9. These are the migrants who work temporarily for one boss, but who travel the whole country working the year round.

10. Although workers may be required to pack any export vegetable, the main crop is red tomatoes, which must be carefully selected and handled. Cucumber, zucchini and others are relatively easier to pack.

11. The use of the notion of average wage is a little arbitrary given that in each case wage differences were found and in two instances wages were higher. In the peak period wages are higher in the capital-intensive regions and the small producers pay more than the larger ones.

References

Acevedo Conde, Maria Luisa (1982) *Desempleo y subempleo rural en los Valles Centrales de Oaxaca.* SEP-INAH, Mexico City.

Arizpe, Lourdes (1985)*Campesinado y Migración.* SEP-CULTURA, Mexico City.

Bidegain, G. Ana Maria (1991) 'Feminización de la pobreza y economía global. Una aproximación desde la historia'. In *Fem*, no. 169, July.

Botey, C., M. Zepeda and L. Heredia (1977) 'Los jornaleros agrícolas migrantes'. Secretaria de la Reforma Agraria, Dirección General de Planeación, Departimento de Estudios Sociales.

Calava, Jose Luis (1991) Conferencia sobre el ejido. Facultad de Economia, UNAM, 14 November.

CIDE (1985) 'Empleo, desempleo y mercados de trabajo. Economía de América Latina'. In *Centro de economia trasnacional*, no. 13, CIDE.

Comision Nacional de los Salarios Minimos (1989) *Compendio de Indicadores de Empleo y Salarios.* December.

Corona, Vazquez Rodrigo (1987) 'Un método para estimar la migración neta definitiva al interior y exterior de diversas areas geográficas'. *Aportes de investigación*, no. 11. CRIM, UNAM.

Las Cuentas Nacionales. 1985–86 and 1986–88, INEGI.

Garcia, Brigida (1988) *Desarrollo económico y absorción de fuerza de trabajo en México. 1950–1980*. El Colegio de México.

Instituto Nacional de Estadisticas, Geografía e Informatica (1986) 'Estudios sobre la mujer (2) Salud Trabajo domestico y Participación social y política'. Serie de lecturas III. Mexico City.

O.I.T. (1985) 'Desempleo y pobreza en un mundo en crisis'. Informe de una reunion de expertos eminentes en cuestiones de empleo.

—— (1988) *Anuario de Estadísticas del Trabajo*.

Quintanilla, Ernesto (1991) 'Tendencias recientes de la localización en la industria maquiladora'. In *Revista de Comercio Exterior*, vol. 41, no. 9, September.

Ramirez, Elia and Hilda Davila (1990) *Trabajo femenino y crisis en México. Tendencias y transformaciones actuales*. UAM-X. January.

Rendon, Teresa (1982) 'El empleo en México: Tendencias Recientes'. *Revista de Investigación Económica*. July–September.

Rendon, Teresa and Carlos Salas (1987) 'Evolución del empleo en México: 1895–1980'. In *Estudios Demográficos y Urbanos*, no. 5, May–August. El Colegio de México.

Roldan, Martha (1982) 'Subordinación genérica y proletarización rural: Un estudio de caso en el noroeste mexicano'. In Leon Magdalena (ed.)*Las trabajadoras del agro*, Vol. II. ACEP, Bogota, Colombia.

Salle, Maria Angeles and Jose Ignacio Casas (1986) *Efectos de la crisis económica sobre el trabajo de las mujeres*. Instituto de la Mujer. Serie Estudios No. 5, Madrid.

Secretaria de Agricultura y Recursos Hidráulicos (SARH) (1986) 'Propuesta de proyecto para el taller sobre formulación y diseño de proyectos para apoyar a las mujeres rurales en actividades de la producción para alimentos'. December. Mexico City.

—— (1988) 'Estadísticas básicas 1960–1986 para la planeación del desarrollo rural integral'. Vol. I, *Sector agropecuario y forestal*. SARH, Subsecretaría de Planeación.

—— (1993)'Coordinación General de Servicios de apoyo a la Producción'. Direccion General de Desarrollo Agroindustrial. Programa a Mediano Plazo para el Desarrollo Agroindustrial en el Estado de Jalisco 1988–93.

Union Nacional de Productores de Hortalizas (UNPH) (1987) XVII Convención anual y XXVIII Asamblea general ordinaria. November.

—— (1989) XIX Convención anual y XXX Asamblea general ordinaria. November.

United Nations (1989) 'Informe sobre la situación social del mundo'. Departamento de Asuntos Economicos y Sociales Internacionales. New York.

Vanackere, Martine (1988) 'Situación de los jornaleros agrícolas en México'. *Revista de Investigacion Económica*, no. 185. July–September.

Zapata, Francisco (1991) 'Tendencias generales y cambios recientes en el mercado de trabajo urbano'. Paper presented at the seminar on labour markets. Colegio de México, Mexico City. October.

Women and the State: Some Considerations of Ideological and Economic Frameworks in Engendering Policies

Haleh Afshar

This brief chapter aims to extend the criticism made of male bias in economics (see Elson and Palmer in Afshar and Dennis, 1992; Bakker, Chapter 1 in this volume) by emphasizing the pervasive role of ideology in constraining women and their access to power and resources. It is the contention here that overarching state ideologies in many countries, and the specific ideologies concerning women and their place in society that are embedded in most, if not all, religions, play an important part in determining policy and selection of priorities at the national level. This means that despite radically different economic approaches to external trade, loan and foreign-exchange policies, and internal social provisions, we can find unexpected similarities in the ideological definition of women's roles in countries as different as Chile and Iran. We also observe unexpected costs and benefits for women of differing classes resulting, unintentionally, from certain government policies. This takes place in the context of states which, regardless of their adherence to economic liberalization or otherwise, maintain a firm political grip and are able to dictate and enforce their political priorities. In this respect, a comparison between Iran and Chile[1] enables us to make some interesting observations.

Restructuring, ideology and gender relations: Chile and Iran

Chile experienced a military coup in the 1970s and embraced the shift towards export-oriented production and the move away from state provisions for health and welfare. The middle classes were the intended beneficiaries of the promised economic boom. By contrast, Iran had an 'anti-imperialist' revolution in 1979 and went to war with Iraq; segregated the sexes in its educational institutions; increased expenditure on health; and claimed to have cut 'dependent relations' with international markets. Food was rationed, and there was an attempt to favour the poorer slum-dwellers, who were seen as the bastions of support for the Islamic regime. Both states adopted a glorified view of motherhood and female domesticity and found support for this among politically vocal middle-class women. Chile adopted a pro-natalist position. The Iranian government initially cut back on free family-planning provisions, but in the latter part of the 1980s embarked on a population-control propaganda campaign.

Mainstream analysts expect to find somewhat lower levels of participation in the labour markets for Chilean women, given the severe erosion of state-backed welfare, which provided both service and employment for them. By contrast, the massive carnage at the front in Iran's eight-year war against Iraq, as well as the revolution's commitment to 'care' for the family, should have led to a rise in the levels of female employment and some improvement in the lives of the poorest women in society. But the belief that women belong to the private sphere and must remain invisible, which is a mainstay of religious and state ideology in Iran, severely eroded any benefits that the expressed intentions of welfarism and the active engagement of men at the war fronts might have brought women. They have ended up in a worse position than Chilean women, who were at least not officially hindered from participating in the labour market.

The military government in Chile embarked on the liberalization programme early and wholeheartedly and could, by 1980, make some spectacular claims. The country increased its volume of exports by a factor of four between 1973 and 1988; this was to an extent based on its diversification of agriculture, which remained the main export sector but produced a more varied cash crop. Chile reduced its dependence on debt (Waylan, 1992: 154). At the same time, there were severe cuts in expenditure on public-sector employment. Women suffered because they had previously been 'encouraged' by the government to work in the suitable areas of nursing (93 per cent of whom were women in 1982) and teaching (75 per cent women in 1982) (Waylan, 1992: 159). An estimated eight thousand were left jobless in one year (1987) alone (Waylan, 1992: 159).

It is well known that a fall in the rate of women's participation in the formal labour market is usually accompanied by a rise in their participation in the informal labour market. At the same time, the lower incomes and poorer employment conditions intensify demand on women's work and time. Less money compels women to cut back on food, to buy poorer-quality food which often requires more processing, and to buy less food more frequently, which means more journeys to and from the market. In addition, retraction of welfare provisions demands more political activity and better organization on the part of women in order to gain access to what little state provisions remain (see Moser, 1992, for detailed discussion). However, despite intensification of the burdens placed on women, and increases in the demands on their time, it was largely the better-paid professional women whose participation rate fell, while that of the poorer women increased. This latter group cut back on the numbers of children they had, and used their low wage rates to compete effectively in the labour market. According to Waylan, there was a 63 per cent increase in the number of economically active women between 1982 and 1987 compared to 12 per cent for men over the same period (Waylan, 1992: 161). Disaggregated data indicate that the poorer women underwent the fastest increase in terms of employment; however, their job gains have been in the worse-paid and least privileged categories of employment. So, in terms of quality of life and ability to fulfil their reproductive roles in a rewarding way, poorer women have lost out. Nevertheless, in terms of access to a wage and to active political participation, the poorer women in Chile did make some gains. As Waylan notes, the combination of authoritarianism and market liberalization increased women's hardship as well as the employment opportunities for some of them; the result was not the hoped-for depoliticization, but a new phase of women's collective organizing (Waylan, 1992: 178).

This is in stark contrast with the experiences of Iranian women, who were promised glorified domesticity and motherhood by the state, but had to achieve it through the intermediary of men (see Afshar, 1991, for further discussion). The Iranian government's gender-segregation policies should have led to a marked increase in the numbers of women employed in health and education.[2] Furthermore, the eight-year war against Iraq should have resulted in an increased participation of women in various industrial and service-sector jobs, and particularly in agriculture, given the large numbers of rural men who had been rounded up and sent to the front. Female employment opportunities did indeed rise markedly in Iraq; women from other Arab countries migrated there in order to benefit from the increased work opportunities (see, for example, Hejab, 1988; Afshar, 1991).

In Iran, the percentage of female public-sector employees almost doubled, from just over 8 per cent of the total in 1966 to 16 per cent in 1988. However, much of this increase occurred *before* the revolution; from 1976 to 1986 the increase was a mere 2 per cent.[3] As the state agencies proliferated, with revolutionary organs doubling up and performing tasks similar to the state bureaucracy, the actual numbers of women civil servants rose from 250,000 to 408,000 between 1976 and 1986. But the rate of increase in the percentage of women civil servants is much slower than that of men. The bulk of the increase was in education, which employed 86 per cent of female public-sector workers. This may be a reflection of the Islamic republic's policy of gender segregation. Since there is an insistence that all public services should be segregated, there is an immediate doubling of the labour force in certain sectors such as health and education. But the policy of sexual segregation also led to a demand by male nurses for a 50 per cent increase in their numbers, to enable them to attend to male patients! That represents an increase in the very sectors that adjustment policies are cutting back elsewhere.

Also, the increase in public-sector employment of women has been more than offset by the dramatic fall in their employment in the private sector. The war coincided with a dramatic fall in the economic activities of the private sector in Iran and a 75 per cent cut back in the numbers of women it employed. The percentage of employed women in the total labour force fell from 14 per cent of the total to 9 per cent in the period 1976–86; and this was despite a lowering of the official age for formal participation in census counts from ten to six! At the same time, there was a six-fold increase in the numbers of officially unemployed women actively seeking paid work. An unexpected consequence of female unemployment was the rapid rise in the birth rate, currently 3.9 per cent per annum, which makes Iran's one of the fastest-growing populations in the world.

What is worth noting is that in Chile, a government long committed to free-market policy and determined to cut back on welfare, has still operated special programmes to provide minimum employment and to help heads of households, who are often women. By contrast, the revolutionary state of Iran has had no systematic welfare provisions or unemployment benefits, despite a commitment in the Constitution to provide for the poor and the needy. In the classic monetarist mode, the best that the destitutes can hope for is charitable hand-outs. In fact, a recent study found that the rational choice for impoverished women was to get themselves jailed, since the best assistance was provided by the charity which supports the dependants of prisoners (Afshar, 1989). At the same time, severe shortages of food, fuel and clothing, and the failure of the government to honour the allocation of rations, has meant that Iranian women, like Chileans, have to spend a great deal of time buying smaller quantities of poorer food and more time and energy processing it into acceptable meals. The burdens of poverty and domesticity are as intense for the impoverished Iranian women, despite the rhetoric of the government, as they are for Chileans. But whereas the poorer Chilean women have more opportunities for paid employment, albeit at low wages, poor Iranian women have almost none. A survey of industrial employment in the Central province in 1988 indicated that no factory had taken on new women workers for a decade (Afshar, 1989).

Conclusion

Both Chile and Iran publicly demanded that women be confined to the domestic sphere. But the Islamic fundamentalists in Iran, by insisting on the segregation of the labour market, have imposed unemployment on a large percentage of women. In this case, the regulation of women via religious notions of domesticity has occurred despite its costs to overall macro-economic performance. By contrast, in the Chilean case, it is the better-trained and educated women who have suffered more from restructuring measures, since the gendered dimension of the labour market is implicit rather than legally enforced. The increased burden on women due to liberalization (expanding women's unpaid labour while also drawing them into the labour market) was in direct contradiction to the military's ideology that women should remain confined to the domestic sphere. In Iran, it is the more educated women who have had some opportunities of benefiting from the upward spiral in the numbers of civil servants and government expenditure on education. Curiously, each government's policies have unintentionally benefited the group least likely to support it politically (in Iran, middle-class women; in Chile, poorer women), and birth rates have gone in the opposite direction to each government's stated wishes: rising in Iran and falling in Chile. Similarly, despite their stated policies, the economic liberalizers have proved to have had better welfare facilities than the revolutionary government of Iran. I suggest that in some respects, religious ideology has had a marked impact in creating these curious results.

Notes

1. The information on Chile is based entirely on Waylan, 1992.
2. Some observers firmly predicted such an outcome: see for example, Moghadam, 1990.
3. Based on the census data published by the Statistical Centre of Iran.

References

Afshar, Haleh (1989) 'Women in the Work and Poverty Trap in Iran'. In H. Afshar and B. Agarwal (eds) *Women, Poverty and Ideology in Asia*. Macmillan, Basingstoke.

———— (1991) 'Fundamentalism and Its Female Apologists'. In I. Pendergast and H. Singer (eds) *Development Perspectives for the 1990s*. Macmillan, Basingstoke.

Afshar, Haleh and Carolyne Dennis (eds) (1992) *Women and Adjustment in the Third World*. Macmillan, London.

Elson, Diane (1992) 'Male Bias in Structural Adjustment'. In H. Afshar and C. Dennis (eds) *Women and Adjustment in the Third World*. Macmillan, Basingstoke.

Hejab, Nadia (1988) *Womanpower*. Cambridge University Press, Cambridge.

Moghadam, Valentine (1990) 'The Reproduction of Gender Inequality in Islamic Societies: A Case Study of Iran in the 1980s'. In *World Development*, vol. 18.

Moser, Caroline (1992) 'Adjustment from Below: Low Income Women, Time and Triple Role in Guayaquail, Ecuador'. In H. Afshar and C. Dennis (eds) *Women and Adjustment in the Third World*. Macmillan, Basingstoke.

Palmer, Ingrid (1992) 'Gender Equity and Economic Efficiency in Adjustment Programmes'. In H. Afshar and C. Dennis (eds) *Women and Adjustment in the Third World*. Macmillan, Basingstoke.

Waylan, Georgina (1992) 'Women, Authoritarianism and Market Liberalisation in Chile, 1973–89'. In H. Afshar and C. Dennis (eds) *Women and Adjustment in the Third World*. Macmillan, Basingstoke.

The Impact of Structural Adjustment Policies on Women: Some General Observations Relating to Conceptual Bias

Swapna Mukhopadhyay

Bias in macro-economics?

The majority of contributors to this volume have argued that macro-economic policies are intentionally or unintentionally imbued with male bias (see especially Bakker, Chapter 1, and Elson, Chapter 2). This brief chapter will cast a somewhat different light on the discussion suggesting that the social context rather than the economic concepts themselves are to blame for gender bias in policy outcomes. I shall also briefly highlight the example of home-working as a distributional scenario resulting from economic policy changes at the macro-level. Marginalization resulting from structural adjustment measures, it is argued, points to both the need for policy intervention and the necessity of micro-level studies that complement our understanding of mechanisms at the macro-level.

What are these macro-economic concepts that are identified as being 'imbued with a male bias'? Presumably, they are concepts like national income, trade balance, investment, money supply – concepts which are the regular fare for any standard course in macro-economics. These concepts are seen to be biased because macro-policies formulated within a framework based on such concepts, while appearing to be gender-neutral, in fact have a discriminatory effect on women. Without going into the question of empirical verification, let us try to unravel the inner logic of such a position.

One aspect of such a logic has to do with the fact that such concepts relate only to market relationships and bypass the private or the domestic sphere. Since the power relations and workloads within the family are tilted against the woman, concepts that relate only to the public sphere will never capture the impact of such inequities that persist outside it. To cite an example: estimates of national income will system-atically exclude the value of housework done primarily by women.

A second dimension of this argument could be that even within the market sector, especially in the labour market, the cards are stacked against women. Women are crowded into the lowest positions in job hierarchies, having a lion's share of the most vulnerable, unprotected and irregular jobs. A policy to improve the trade balance under struc-tural adjustment might involve subtle changes in contractual arrange-ments in the labour market, resulting in overall vulnerability of the workforce – a phenomenon that has been recorded under such pro-grammes in many countries in recent times.[1] The differential adverse impact of such changes on women might be significantly more pro-nounced, but unless gender-differences in such matters are specifically monitored, one would not even be aware of the seriousness of the impact. Similarly, a fall in employment may hit women harder, because it is they who are crowded into less protected and more irregular jobs to start with.

A third plank of the argument could involve the shifting balance between the private and the public domains under different policy regimes (see Brodie, Chapter 3 in this volume). For instance, if structural adjustment programmes result in a shrinkage of the extent of public-sector involvement in the provision of social services – an apprehension that has been voiced by many – the responsibility for providing such services will then devolve onto the private sphere, and hence, given the prevailing social modes, disproportionately onto women. If the macro-concepts and macro-policies do not register the differential impact of policy changes that are detrimental to women, then – the argument goes – the bias has to lie in the concepts.

Such an argument appears to be faulty on a number of counts. From the point of view of pure deductive logic, faulty concepts may be suf-ficient to generate faulty conclusions, but not all faulty conclusions need be the result of faulty concepts. In this particular case, we believe the fault lies not so much with the concepts as such but with the fact that the social environment is biased against women: that there is often a lack of gender-disaggregated information, resulting from an absence of awareness, and hence a failure to monitor the differential impact of policy changes at various levels, both within and outside the public sphere. If certain macro-policies do have gender-discriminatory fallouts, it is the job of the concerned scholars and policy-makers to chart such impacts and suggest remedial action. Besides, one must realize that discrimination has many faces. Economic policies may have a similar discriminatory impact on the young or the old, on specific ethnic groups or on minorities; in India, on Scheduled Castes and Scheduled Tribes.

How does one design 'concepts' and 'policies' that will have a neutral, homogeneous impact on all such groups in the economy?

Merging the private and the public domains

A more pertinent issue relates to the question of the division of work organization and role specifications between the private and the public domains and the implications of such differences for policy. Without invoking the historical origins of such partitioning of domains of activity and its linkage with the status of women, one can perhaps say that this division and the associated gender-typing of roles are symptoms of the fundamental malady characterizing patriarchal society. It is clear that if the public and private domains are indeed separated in practice, the macro-concepts that relate only to the former will, indeed, continue to have limited applicability. What is important is that the gender-disaggregated implication of such a limitation is clearly recognized.

All concepts are, in a manner of speaking, necessarily limited by the boundaries of their definitions. Thus the possibility of bias in the *use* of any conceptual framework is ingrained in the essence of such delimitation: clearly the extent of bias will depend on the context of its use. In the final analysis, it is a trade-off between the errors involved in changing the boundaries of the definition and those involved in keeping them unchanged. In this particular case, so long as the principles of production, exchange and co-ordination within the domestic sphere are different from those outside it, there is a justification in having separate sets of concepts for the two spheres; although, as all social scientists know, such separation is never complete, that there are bound to be fuzzy zones in between. However, segregating the two in no way precludes the need, or the possibility, of analysing the impact of changes in the public sphere on the relations within the domestic sphere, or vice versa.

Consider the obverse side of this issue. Supposing we did have a set of concepts that were not 'male-biased', one criterion they would need to satisfy would be that they would have to relate to the private as well as to the public domain. To take the example previously cited, that estimates of national income would have to include the imputed value of women's housework: without getting into the thorny problem of how to go about fixing the imputed value of housework,[2] what is it that we can expect from such a reformulation? In my judgement, nothing very substantive. The message that women bear the brunt of domestic chores worldwide could be equally well, if not better articulated by properly designed time-allocation studies. If social norms in gender-typing of roles persist, no amount of juggling with concepts and measurements would be able to cure the 'male bias'. The solution lies, not in throwing away the existing conceptual framework lock, stock and barrel, but in monitoring and analysing the gender-differentiated impact of macro-policies within and outside the market. For, the problem as I perceive it lies in investing the macro-concepts and the macro-policies *per se* with a gender bias, whereas in reality the bias lies in the socio-economic environment within which such policies are applied. It is important to demarcate the two clearly, not merely for the sake of conceptual clarity but also in order to be able to design effective policy interventions to counter such bias.

Structural adjustment and stabilization measures: are they woman-friendly?

To illustrate the point, let us first look at what these macro-economic measures entail. As has been discussed in the Introduction to this volume (Chapter 1), structural adjustment measures are usually aimed at altering the long-run growth dynamics of an economy by operating on the supply side, while stabilization relates to curtailing excess demand in order to reduce current deficits in external accounts and to contain price inflation in the domestic sector. The usual structural adjustment measures consist of allowing for greater 'free market' operations, greater privatization, de-licensing, introduction of uniform tax and tariff structures, abolition of price and import controls, abolition of subsidies and promotion of what has come to be known as labour-market flexibility; while the usual tools used for stabilization consist of domestic credit squeeze, curtailment of budgetary deficits, reduction in money supply, and devaluation.

One way of reacting to such macro-policy measures would be to support those that seem to be gender-neutral or 'woman friendly' on application and oppose those that are not. To take an example: by this logic all privatization measures are to be denigrated if employment conditions for women on average are perceived to be better in the public sector than in the private sector, even if the former entails indefinite subsidization of sick or inefficient public-sector units. An alternative approach would be to decide on the privatization issue on general economic principles, which would undoubtedly throw up different answers in different cases depending on the specifications of the case concerned, while working for better terms and conditions of employment for women in the private sector through such supplementary programmes as better access to skills training for women, greater awareness and improved labour-market information-dissemination mechanisms. If one were to decide on the privatization issue on the sole criterion of gender bias, one might tend to ignore more compelling specificities and end up making a decision that could hurt the overall growth performance of the economy in the long run, with consequent adverse implications for everybody, including women. It pays to locate the fault clearly where it belongs, for otherwise one might end up throwing away the baby with the proverbial bath-water.

To make a general point, a macro-policy measure that may be desirable from the point of view of the economy might appear to be discriminatory towards women, while one that is woman-friendly could be a bad policy for the system as a whole. Often it could be self-defeating to denigrate the former and support the latter, for the simple reason that women as workers, home-makers and consumers are part of the whole system, and a policy regime that hurts the economic system in the large is unlikely to lead to betterment of women's conditions on a sustainable basis. Thus, while it is imperative to monitor the impact of various economic policies on the condition of women and to try to counter their male bias, it may not often be a good policy to make a judgement on the desirability or otherwise of a macro-policy measure solely on the basis of its observed, or perceived, impact on women.

Having said this, there is a perfectly valid reason why there exists a general feeling of worry and consternation about the impact of structural adjustment policies on all marginalized groups, including women. These measures, as they stand, have nothing explicit to say about issues such as poverty and unemployment. They figure nowhere in the central focus of concerns. It is presumed that if and when imbalances do get corrected, and growth picks up, such problems will get sorted out on their own: almost a modern version of the old 'trickle-down' hypothesis. The worry is that if the whole gamut of measures to stabilize, liberalize and privatize the economies leads to lopsided growth, and if public disinvestment leads to the erosion of the already meagre state provision of social services and infrastructural facilities, one could end up with a distributional scenario that is actually far worse than what one had started off with. In a situation like this, women who are highly concentrated in the bottom rungs of most hierarchies would clearly be the relative losers. The issues involved can be illustrated with the help of a specific form of production organization mainly involving women workers, which is reportedly on the rise in developing countries going in for massive doses of structural adjustment.

Home-based work and women

Home-based work is work done exclusively for a person (middleman) or an agency, normally within the precincts of the worker's homestead but in any case unsupervised by the employer. Payment is generally piece-rated. No clear employer–employee relationships can be established, so that usual labour laws covering wage workers are inapplicable, often *de jure*, and almost always *de facto*. Much of the increase in the incidence of home-based work in developing countries in recent times is ascribed to women workers. From the employers' point of view, such a form of production organization is attractive as it allows for a high degree of flexibility in labour use – shedding workers when demand slackens off and absorbing them from virtually a reserve army when it does tighten up. From the home-workers' point of view, the ability to participate in the market economy without having to go through the rigours of regular working hours away from home is attractive on two counts. The flexibility in time and place of work allows them – mostly women – to continue to look after their domestic chores, which the society has ordained is their primary responsibility. At the same time, for those inexorably dragged onto the bottom rungs of the market economy by a whole range of factors, the opportunity to earn some ready cash is always welcome. To the extent that technology allows fragmentation of the production process, home-based work, on the face of it, appears to be a Pareto-optimal form of work organization. It is small wonder, then, that the phenomenon is on the rise all over the Third World, in activities ranging from garment-making, embroidery, food processing, and beedi-rolling, to anything such as assembling components in the electrical-appliances industry.

Such an account, however, does not reveal the conditions under which the home-based worker normally operates, or is compelled to operate. On top of insecurity of income, the isolation of workers from one another precludes possibilities of systematic information exchange or organizational efforts, so that rates of remuneration for work performed are usually abominably low. Since the compulsion to participate in the market economy is often spurred on by the forced commercialization of erstwhile peasant farmers, or erstwhile housewives from poor urban families hit by recession or technology-induced unemployment,[3] the major apprehension in this context is that structural adjustment policies might lead to further deterioration in the working conditions of women where the brunt of flexibility will have to be borne mainly by these vulnerable groups.

Redirecting policy

At the macro-policy level, it is therefore important to highlight the need to redirect public resources towards the social sectors in a more effective manner. Efforts could be directed towards pressing for woman-oriented development programmes in health and nutrition, and designing appropriate incentives to promote female literacy. Vocational training for women is another area which needs to be operationalized. However, to understand the genesis of, and mutations in the processes of marginalization set about by, structural adjustment measures, one needs to depend heavily on micro-studies. Such processes could be mediated through new forms of work organization (for example, the emergence of home-based work as a device for drawing on the atomized labour of the Third World 'housewife' in the national and international capitalist systems), through new technology (for example, the gender-discriminatory impact of the power loom in the textile sector in India, or the impact of micro-chip technology on the labour-use pattern of women in Canada), or through new structures of access to resources. Micro-studies that probe into the manner in which such processes affect the work and lives of women are essential for designing appropriate policy interventions, at the macro-level, as well as at the sectoral level.

Notes

1. See the *World Labour Report*, Vol. III (1989), International Labour Organization, Geneva.

2. Evaluating housework, especially where the market for housework does not exist, poses enormous analytical and empirical problems. Nevertheless, there have been a number of attempts to measure the contribution of household work to income. See Goldschmidt-Clermont, 1985 for a survey of empirical exercises, and Swapna Mukhopadhyay, 'The Nature of Household Work' (mimeo), Institute of Economic Growth (1982), for the analytical issues involved.

3. See Mukhopadhyay (forthcoming) for an analysis of macro-policy-induced changes in labour market conditions with special reference to home-based work in the developing countries in recent times.

References

Goldschmidt-Clermont, Luisella (1985) *Unpaid Work in the Household: A Review of Economic Evaluation Methods*. ILO, Geneva.

Mies, Maria, Veronika Bennholdt-Thomson and Claudia Von Werlhof (1988) *Women – The Last Colony*. Zed Books, London.

Mukhopadhyay, Swapna (forthcoming) *From Isolation to Empowerment: Women Home-Based Workers in the Less Developed Countries*. ILO, Geneva.

Index